UNSTUCK

UNSTUCK

Engaging in Spiritual Conversations

STEVE SHORES

WIPF & STOCK · Eugene, Oregon

UNSTUCK
Engaging in Spiritual Conversations

Copyright © 2022 Steve Shores. All rights reserved. Except for brief quotations in critical publications or reviews, no part of this book may be reproduced in any manner without prior written permission from the publisher. Write: Permissions, Wipf and Stock Publishers, 199 W. 8th Ave., Suite 3, Eugene, OR 97401.

Wipf & Stock
An Imprint of Wipf and Stock Publishers
199 W. 8th Ave., Suite 3
Eugene, OR 97401

www.wipfandstock.com

PAPERBACK ISBN: 978-1-6667-9053-5
HARDCOVER ISBN: 978-1-6667-9051-1
EBOOK ISBN: 978-1-6667-9052-8

05/23/22

Unless otherwise noted, Scripture quotations taken from the (NASB®) New American Standard Bible®, Copyright © 1960, 1971, 1977, 1995, 2020 by The Lockman Foundation. Used by permission. All rights reserved. www.lockman.org.

All stories from my counseling practice have been modified to protect privacy and confidentiality.

Dedicated to Sonya Reeder and Dale McDiarmid, both of whom model beautifully what it means to engage in rich, spiritual conversations.

I would have despaired unless I had believed
that I would see the goodness of the Lord /
In the land of the living. (Ps 27:13)

Contents

Preface ix

Acknowledgments xi

Introduction xiii

Chapter 1 Three Questions Crucial to Spiritual Conversations 1

Chapter 2 Listening 27

Chapter 3 The Storied Self 33

Chapter 4 Spiritual Conversations and Kingdom 40

Chapter 5 How Does the Helper Help? 53

Chapter 6 The Facets of Trouble 68

Chapter 7 Traumatic Stress 82

Chapter 8 What I Have Learned as a Helper 88

Conclusion 91

Bibliography 93

Preface

The epigraph from Ps 27:13 notes that the psalmist's plunge toward despair was arrested by faith: "I believed that I would see the goodness of the Lord / In the land of the living." In my career both as a counselor in private practice and in hundreds of spiritual conversations outside my office, I've had to face the obvious, sad fact that people are carrying heavy loads and are often internally screaming under the weight. They experience the "land of the living" more as a dying than not. I've learned an equally great and more hopeful truth: so often, "the goodness of the Lord" reaches into "the land of the living" only because one person is willing to engage the other's hurting soul in the kind of hopeful, bracing interaction that, in this book, I call "spiritual conversation."

The nature of a spiritual conversation will become clear in the pages to come. Here, I think it crucial to establish that these conversations form the enactment—the carrying into the world—of the theology of relational discipleship developed in the first three volumes. Without making it an official title, I've often thought of these four books as The Relationship Project, for through the actions of love, "all men will know that you are My disciples" (John 13:35). Elevating the question of how we relate to others to the first rank of theology has been the attempt of the first three volumes. They have sought to make relationships central to discipleship. This last volume is an effort to show how discipleship is carried into the world through relationships in the form of spiritual conversations.

Acknowledgments

Under this heading, my thoughts turn to the hundreds of counselees who have blessed me with their trust over the years. By opening their lives in such unstinting ways, they have taught me the essential roles played by risk and vulnerability in the journey of discipleship. I have been a sometimes-middling student in their master class of courage and patience.

I would like to thank Kara Barlow, my copy editor. I'm grateful that she has consistently provided a wise and clarifying perspective. Not to mention an eye for detail that I lack. These books would be much the poorer without her.

I dedicated the first book of this series to my wife, Susan. Here, I extend that dedication to say that she has initiated and been open to more spiritual conversations than I can shake a stick at. I'm infinitely improved by these (also risky and vulnerable) talks over the years. They, too, have been instances of "the goodness of the Lord in the land of the living." Thank you, Susan. You are the marrow of these books.

Introduction

This is a book about getting unstuck through spiritual conversations. The first three books of this series have focused on how we get stuck in our too-small stories of self-made survival; how stuck-ness causes suffering in relationships in contradiction to Jesus' command to "love one another"; how repentance restores relationships; and how waiting for the maturity to repent (in ourselves and others) is a form of long-suffering that God uses to foster the very maturity for which we hope. Now, we come more fully to the relational dimension of maturing. How can two people connect by engaging in spiritual conversations that create a salutary pull toward growth in the one seeking help?

That question raises another: How am I using the term "spiritual conversation"? Let's start with the idea of conversation. The literal meaning of "converse" is to go back and forth (with), as can be seen from the Latin, *verso*, which means "to turn hither and thither."[1] The to-and-fro of conversing suggests the concept of a true exchange of thoughts, feelings, and questions between any two parties. The word "true" in the previous sentence means that domination, manipulation, or withdrawal play an ever-decreasing part in a real conversation, especially on the part of the one I will, throughout this book, call "the helper" (more on that later). Domination, manipulation, and withdrawal act as clogs in the flow of connecting. If a pack of dogs ran against the flow of a fast break in basketball, the effect would be similar.

---

1. Marchant and Charles, *Cassell's Latin Dictionary*, 613.

INTRODUCTION

What happens when we add the word "spiritual" to "conversations"? Of course, spiritual derives from "spirit," which can be an uncomfortably nebulous word unless we settle it within the sphere of the Holy Spirit. This is the third person of the Trinity and the one to whom Jesus refers when he says, "The wind blows where it wishes and you hear the sound of it, but do not know where it comes from and where it is going; so is every one who is born of the Spirit" (John 3:8). In the New Testament, this Spirit-wind is *pneuma*, and in the Old Testament, it is *rûach*. The latter term means breeze, breath, or wind, with special reference to the "breath that gives life."[2] Another author points out that "it is the 'wind' which proceeds from Yahweh and returns to him that also constitutes the breath of man's life."[3] The third person of the Trinity, then, governs the animation of all life, as intimated in Ps 104:29-30: "Thou dost hide Thy face, they are dismayed; / Thou dost take away their spirit, they expire, / And return to their dust. / Thou dost send forth Thy Spirit, they are created; / And Thou dost renew the face of the ground." As used in this book, spiritual conversations reflect the Holy Spirit's interest in sparking in us new motivations for life, for coming alive into new freedoms that leave behind self-protective rigidities. A spiritual conversation, then, is *a real exchange of thoughts, feelings, questions, and struggles in a progressively less defensive, progressively more honest effort to follow the Holy Spirit's lead in releasing new life.* Such an exchange coheres well with Anderson's emphasis on one person helping another find motivation to grow.[4]

Earlier, I mentioned the word "helper." I have settled on this important word as a key element of connecting relationally. Spiritual conversations, to be helpful, must bear in mind the question "Helpful with what?" We began to home in on this question with the previous paragraph's italicized definition. There, we ended with the phrase "releasing new life." The helper, then, progressively develops the capacity to act as the Holy Spirit's ally in fostering new life in others. The helper, of course, cannot actually foster that life. Rather,

---

2. Koehler et al., *Hebrew and Aramaic Lexicon*, 1197-99.
3. Wolff, *Anthropology*, 33.
4. Anderson, *Christians Who Counsel*, 71-72.

INTRODUCTION

he or she acts to create conditions conducive to new life, conditions that constitute space for the Spirit to work.

We can begin to understand what I mean by "new life" by taking note of Jesus' words in John 6:63: "It is the Spirit who gives life; the flesh profits nothing; the words that I have spoken to you are spirit and are life." The word "flesh" here denotes "unaided human nature . . . which is absolutely impotent in the things of God."[5] Jesus reserves spiritual impact for himself and the Holy Spirit: "[This verse] tells us how God's Spirit *gets to* human beings: through Jesus' words. And, reciprocally, it tells us how God's Word *gets into* human beings: through the Spirit using Jesus [sic] words. Today's English Version translates our text's sense well: 'My words bring the life-giving Spirit.'"[6] The role of the helper, then, consists of facilitating an atmosphere in which the Spirit can reach into another's life with the perspectives of Jesus. Or, to put it another way, with those of the kingdom of God. And, since "God so loved the world that He gave . . ." (John 3:16), a key value of God's kingdom will be growth in self-giving love.

Now, we can see that the role of helper assumes an objective of discipleship in the context of John 13:35: "By this all men will know that you are My disciples, if you have love for one another." This is a book about how spiritual conversations might foster growth in the kind of love Jesus has in mind. Learning this kind of love *is* a release of new life. What kind of love does Jesus have in mind? The previous verse touches the heart of it: "A new commandment I give to you, that you love one another, even as I have loved you, that you also love one another" (John 13:34). Oh! "Even as I have loved you" stratospherically raises the bar. Living in this kind of love involves a self-giving that, even on our best days, we glimpse from far distances. Even so, the question remains: What would need to happen in spiritual conversations that might seed this love within one another? In answer, we'll explore four dimensions crucial to spiritual conversations: (1) What is going on inside (in the helper, first, and then the other)? (2) What is God up to? (3) How may the

---

5. Bruner, *Gospel of John*, 448.
6. Bruner, *Gospel of John*, 448, his emphasis.

INTRODUCTION

helper learn to see clearly? (4) How might we use the idea of story to explore more deeply our answers to the first three questions? In the next chapter, we'll wrestle with the first three questions above. A chapter-length interlude about listening comes next. Then, we'll wrestle with answering the fourth question.

CHAPTER 1

Three Questions Crucial to Spiritual Conversations

WHAT IS GOING ON INSIDE?

How *does* a helper actually help when others are mired in perplexity and struggle? A perplexed soul deals with a puzzle he or she can't put together, a wilderness impenetrable, a mystery unsolvable. A helper has to go into the mystery with that beleaguered one. A helper, then, has to go where the person *is*, into the wilderness, and must understand, over time, the issues that confound the soul. "Confound" emerges downstream in the flow of a word history involving the idea of being poured together and thus all mixed up.[1] Life has spilled innumerable encounters, events, and conflicts into the soul, which has become mixed up, confused, and pained. For the helper truly to connect with the other, then, means entering confusion, which entails feeling all the distress that accompanies it.

Imagine, for example, that the one seeking help opens up and says, "I don't understand why God allowed me to live through my accident. You almost couldn't recognize that the car was a car! And, sure, it was a miracle that I lived; but look at me! I'm in a

1. *Complete Wordfinder*, 294.

wheelchair. My disability checks don't nearly cover my part of the bills. The load has fallen on my wife. My kids are sad. I feel like a huge burden. Why am I here?" A new set of contingencies has flooded this man and his family. He can barely tread water in a sea of loss. Suppose the helper, meaning well, says, "That's hard, but you just have to realize that God's in control." The problem here is that, in all likelihood, the struggler already has *some* understanding of the concept of God's sovereignty. In fact, part of his being confounded relates to this very theme: Why didn't God, as the all-powerful sovereign, simply prevent the wreck? The helper's God-in-control stance simply tells the sufferer a confusing and, at this point, unhelpful idea he already knows. I am not intending to impugn God's sovereignty here, only to illustrate how the idea of it can be tossed into a struggler's life from an safe distance, thus becoming just another load to shoulder.

While the idea of God's kingly reign *is* a rich source for perspective change, the helper's deploying it right off the bat raises the question, "Why this choice at this point?" That is, what's the rush? What does this early bid to place the man in the wheelchair into the bubble of God's sovereignty say about the helper? What happened inside to inform the helper's choice to lay the claim of God's rule over the suffering family?

What is Going on Inside the Helper?

The question of what wheels are turning inside the helper is crucial, because they often form potent obstacles to effective listening. The skill of listening—which we'll discuss in the next chapter—rises or falls with the helper's willingness to assess his or her own internal heart traffic. Without a growing understanding of "the hidden person of the heart" (1 Pet 3:4), the helper will foist the offshoots of unresolved internal conflicts onto others. Going back to our example of the one who led with "God is in control," we might surmise a fear of failure (or of chaos) within the helper and a consequent need to exert control by "having an answer." Ironically, "God is in control" may mean "*I* need to feel in control." Here, the problem isn't just

THREE QUESTIONS FOR SPIRITUAL CONVERSATIONS

needing control, but also that one isn't *aware* of the need and how it drives the response to the struggler. The result is that one acts to help not the struggler but oneself. The *helper* ends up with the needed self-assurance, but the struggler is abandoned.

What follows is that for any of us to be helpful to others, *we need help*. That is, we need others who will come alongside, lovingly and prayerfully, to walk us through any hot-button issues that lie dormant inside us. We may need to seek out a counselor or a pastor well versed in people helping. In Ps 51:6, David, in the throes of confessing his sin to God, cries out, "Behold, Thou dost desire truth in the innermost being, / And in the hidden part Thou wilt make me know wisdom." The verse implies that David had been driven to sin with Bathsheba by a *lack* of truth in his heart, resulting in a "hidden part" that steered him awry. Eventually, Nathan the prophet confronted David, courageously becoming his helper. On the other hand, why didn't David seek Nathan *before* he jumped off the cliff and pursued Bathsheba? We all need a "Nathan" to fill the role described in Prov 20:5: "A plan in the heart of a man is like deep water, / But a man of understanding draws it out."

These phrasings:

- unresolved internal conflicts
- truth in the innermost being
- the hidden part
- deep water

convey both the reality and the difficulty of searching for dynamics within the helper that may prevent her from offering real help. Notice that the latter three terms derive from biblical sources (Psalms and Proverbs) while the first emerges from the world of psychological studies, an epistemological corridor that has generated a vast field of data in the last 130 years. The data vary tremendously and must be carefully vetted through the lens of revelational dependency. It's beyond the scope of this book to lay out the parameters of a proper, biblical lens for interpreting the data set of psychology.

UNSTUCK

Suffice it to say that I'll be taking a "spoiling the Egyptians"[2] approach to the world of psychological study and research. Such an approach carefully receives data from psychological studies that does not contradict the Judeo-Christian dependency on Old and New Testament revelation either directly or by implication. For example, the term "unresolved internal conflicts" traces its roots to psychoanalysis and is an attempt to denote the contending of forces within the person (id vs. ego, ego vs. superego, ego vs. reality, etc.). The Bible, on the other hand, does not—either directly or by implication—speak of such conflicts. Rather, it speaks of a different set of conflicts: sin vs. grace, flesh vs. spirit, chaos vs. order, fall vs. redemption, and so on. It will not do simply to try and jam the two worlds together. A historical analysis from a Christian theologian may help us here:

> Although most human beings give the appearance at times of being confused seekers for truth with a naive respect for God, says [Jonathan] Edwards, the reality is that unless they are moved by the Spirit they have a natural distaste for the real God, an uncontrollable desire to break his laws and a constant tendency to sit in judgment on him when they notice him at all. They are at moral enmity with the God revealed in the Bible. Since his purpose crosses theirs at every juncture, they really hate him more than any finite object, and this is clearly displayed in their treatment of his Son.[3]

The same writer, Richard Lovelace, presses on to draw some implications for the loss—in significant swaths of the church—of this depth view of sin in the last couple of centuries:

> During the late nineteenth century, while the church's understanding of the unconscious motivation behind surface actions was vanishing, Sigmund Freud rediscovered this factor and recast it in an elaborate and profound secular mythology. One of the consequences of this remarkable shift is that in the twentieth century pastors have often been reduced to the status of legalistic

2. Crabb, *Effective Biblical Counseling*, 47–56.
3. Lovelace, *Dynamics*, 86.

THREE QUESTIONS FOR SPIRITUAL CONVERSATIONS

moralists, while the deeper aspects of the cure of souls are generally relegated to psychotherapy, even among Evangelical Christians.[4]

Standing on Jonathan Edwards's shoulders, Lovelace crafts a masterful analysis of the church's jettisoning of its rich, biblical heritage of depth theology, ceding it over to a depth psychology that has the merit of retaining the idea of depth but the liability of evaluating humans from a closed-universe perspective that, by definition, excludes revelation from God.

Pulling some threads together here: When I include "unresolved internal conflicts" in the bulleted list on page 3, I'm not suggesting that the whole Freudian corpus waltz in behind, as if the concept is the camel's nose under the tent flap. Rather, since the church *has* lost some of its depth-related vocabulary (for example, John of the Cross's "caverns of the soul"[5]), it seems useful to employ "unresolved internal conflicts" to convey that (1) wars rage in the human heart (we are a people contended over, *and* we contend with ourselves and others); (2) clinical psychology has, by dint of spending millions of hours seeking to connect with hurting souls, glimpsed the idea that unless these wars/conflicts reach some kind of peaceful resolution, the human will remain bound. The compulsive recycling of unresolved inner conflict (another term would be "the war within") confines the human to the old map we discussed in *Cleanup*, the second book in this series.

A bit of autobiography may assist in illustrating these two points. When I was a sophomore in college, my father left my life. As you might expect, I'd been counting on him to be my "North Star" into the adult years that were near at hand. In one night, between Christmas and New Year's (usually a time of cocooning and "peace on earth"), the star vanished, leaving me devastated and disoriented. On top of that, amid the upheaval and shock of our family's dying, Dad asked me and one of my brothers to help move some things to his new apartment. And we complied. Later, I looked back on that compliance with shame. How could I have

---

4. Lovelace, *Dynamics*, 88.
5. John of the Cross, *Living Flame*, 69.

helped him, even briefly, with the dissolution of our family? When the shame of it hit me, I became aware of a longing for mercy on the one hand and, on the other, a critical voice excoriating me deep inside. The cry for mercy was silenced by the whip of rebuke. In my "innermost being," I could not resolve the conflict in my heart, so I tried to ignore it, locking it in a deep compartment where the low-lying hum of shame generated anxiety and sadness. Far above this level of conflict, in my functioning life, I developed a competent, people-pleasing persona that assiduously put people off the scent of shame.

Throughout my twenties, though, about every month or two, I'd fall into what I now know was a mild depression. Not understanding that at the time, I would power through, as if holding in my emotional guts with one hand and "doing life" with the other. I didn't even know it was okay to tell my wife when I was suffering. During the times of powering through (I only know this when I look back), I was strangely distant and quiet. Deeply needing "truth in the innermost being," I staggered on without it, blending times of cheerfulness with morose spells that neither I nor my wife understood.

My heart was at war with itself, the hope of mercy rising and then drowning again in the harsh condemnation: "You helped him! Where was your courage? You should've stood up to him!" Greater than that battle was a still deeper conflict, one in which "our struggle is not against flesh and blood, but against the rulers, against the powers, against the world forces of this darkness, against the spiritual forces of wickedness in the heavenly places" (Eph 6:12). The agenda of the dark forces was to bottle up the new spiritual life within me (I had become a Christian about two months before my father took his exit), paralyzing it in the unresolved bind between mercy and shame. The mocker amplified the accusing voice inside me to such a pitch that, in my torment, I would resort to an old addiction in a bid for relief. Of course, that would only intensify the boil of shame in my exhausted heart. I did not yet know to cry with Paul, "Who will set me free from the body of this death?" (Rom 7:24). I did not yet know Christ on *that* level. I needed a helper who would be willing to come all the way into my wilderness.

THREE QUESTIONS FOR SPIRITUAL CONVERSATIONS

Had that helper never come alongside, my efforts to *be* a helper would have been dotted with pitfalls. Connecting with others who might also be prone to compulsive self-criticism would have pushed my buttons. I might have become reactive, pushing the other toward solutions simply to get the topic to fade. Or, I may have lapsed into a noncommittal listening, politely attending while hoping the other would change the subject. Or, *I* might simply change the topic myself. Had others been unwilling to enter *my* wilderness, helping me work through the inner storm, then the option of moving *into* the other's tendency to self-severity would have been unlikely. I would not have had "ears to hear" (Matt 13:9). I needed "truth in the innermost being" in order to resolve the suppressed war in my heart, thus freeing me to move more readily into the lives of others.

Through the tool of autobiography, we can shed more light on the two points on page 5. First, we noted that the human heart is a place of war. We humans are contended over. Further, we contend with ourselves and with others. The roots of this contention lie in Gen 3, where Satan insidiously questions Adam and Eve's concepts of God, aiming to foster distorted images of God in the human heart. God, in his turn, counters the satanic distortion by revealing truth about himself. The Bible forms the Lord's flanking attack on Satan's lie. The effect is that contradictory models of God collide like cosmic armies. This is the war.

What I mean by our being "contended over" is captured in 1 John 5:19: "But we know that we are of God, and the whole world lies in the power of the evil one." The writer identifies a "we," believers in Jesus Christ, and a "world" that is under the rule of a usurping master. Christians are released from his rule, but he doesn't relinquish them easily. Having lost them through God's having transferred them "out of darkness into His marvelous light" (1 Pet 2:9), he nonetheless seeks to blind them to the glories of their new status and to the machinations of the ingrained patterns in which they walk in the flesh. Satan can't keep them from their being claimed by the light of God, but he can do his scheming best to keep them from being a "city set on a hill" (Matt 5:14). That's why Paul says that the real conflict of life is "not against flesh and blood, but against the rulers, against the powers, against the world forces of this darkness,

7

against the spiritual forces of wickedness in the heavenly places" (Eph 6:12). This universal, subliminal contention can easily lure us into perceiving life as a win-lose, all-or-nothing contest that becomes a zero-sum game with others as our competitors. Thus, we come close to Thomas Hobbes's "war of all against all."[6] The adversarial atmosphere induces us to live tactically, making moves to pry from life the outcomes we deem necessary. But to live so, we must suppress a bad conscience, which becomes part of the "truth" we "suppress . . . in unrighteousness" (Rom 1:28). In the struggle with conscience, we are at war with ourselves.

The first clarification, then, is that wars rage in the human heart. The second is that clinical psychology (i.e., psychology engaged with actual people in therapeutic encounter) has helped demonstrate that unresolved conflict keeps the human bound, like Gulliver in Lilliput. This is perhaps the most important contribution of secular psychology. On the other hand, while psychology functions well by highlighting the *fact* of internal conflict, it does a relatively poor job of showing what that conflict *signifies*. I say this because psychology has an attenuated definition of the very word, *psychē*, that is the genesis of the word "psychology." Clinical psychology speaks of "intrapsychic conflict" (for example, the conflicts among id, ego, and superego, and those between the ego and reality). But, again, the "psychic" in "intrapsychic" is poorly defined. What *is* the *psychē*? In Christian terms, it is the soul. What is the soul? Pastoral counselor Charles Gerkin says:

> The term soul is here used as a theological term that points to the self's central core [which is] subject to the ego's conflicting forces and to the ultimate origins of the self in God. The soul is the gift of God bestowed upon the individual with the breath of life. It is thus the self, including its ego conflicts, as seen from an ultimate perspective—the perspective of the self as nurtured and sustained in the life of God.[7]

Christian philosopher Dallas Willard says:

---

6. Hobbes, *Of Man*, 392.
7. Gerkin, *Living Human Document*, 98.

THREE QUESTIONS FOR SPIRITUAL CONVERSATIONS

> The soul is that dimension of the person that interrelates all of the other dimensions so that they form one life. It is like a meta-dimension or higher-level dimension because its directed field of play consists of the other dimensions (thought, body, and so on), and through them it reaches ever deeper into the person's vast environment of God and his creation.... [It] encompasses and "organizes" the whole person.[8]

Old Testament scholar Hans Walter Wolff, using the Hebrew term for soul, says, "The fact [is] that... [*nephesh*] points pre-eminently to needy man."[9] He goes on to say that human awareness of need emerges in one's orientation to God.[10] If suppressed, it is still true that men and women know that the need they sense—the ache or thirst in the soul, I would call it—can only be met in God. On the other hand, according to Jonathan Barnes, the emphasis of modern psychology is to regard the soul *as* the human mind in a reductive way that is similar to the thought of Descartes.[11] From this point of view, what makes us human is our being a spot of thinking in the vast, empty cosmos. From the biblical data adduced by the first three authors above, it can be seen that this is far too simple—meager on its face—and runs the risk of a mind-body split that destroys the wholeness of the human. The idea of humans as mere thinking spots moves toward eliminating the vast theme of call-and-response that the Bible makes central to the life that is truly human.

What, then, *does* war in the human heart signify? That we are caught between stories, that our lives unfold as narratives, and that those narratives are deeply contested. Again, we traced the heart of the contest to the tension between the self-revelation of God and the distortions of our God-concepts that Satan has infused into the human.

How does this affect the helper? Unless the helper becomes attuned to her distortions about God, the help provided will reflect

---

8. Willard, *Renovation*, 37.
9. Wolff, *Anthropology*, 25.
10. Wolff, *Anthropology*, 25.
11. Barnes, "Psyche."

distorted pictures of the Creator and of his creatures, including the created being across from the helper. Consider:

> In its biblical definition, sin cannot be limited to isolated instances or patterns of wrongdoing; it is something much more akin to the psychological term *complex*: an organic network of compulsive attitudes, beliefs and behavior deeply rooted in our alienation from God. Sin originated in the darkening of the human mind and heart as man turned from the truth about God to embrace a lie about him and consequently a whole universe of lies about his creation.[12]

The chief of all lies (perpetrated by "the father of lies" [John 8:44]) is that, since God's character should be suspected of hidden agendas and self-seeking, we humans are on our own and must become masters of competitive ingenuity. The war with God ("You can't be trusted!") devolves into the war with others over limited resources in a world of scarcity, then devolves further into a war with ourselves in that we uneasily justify to ourselves that our raiding of others is okay (they deserve it, because they strive to have the goods we ourselves "must" have). To the degree that the helper listens from within this competitive mindset, she will be more reactive than helpful *vis-à-vis* others. Tragically, it's also true that the helper will suppress this reactiveness. The indicator that it's present, however, is the helper's giving advice from a comfortable distance.

What is Going on Inside the Other?

A story may shed some light on this question. Recently, someone I've been helping felt a bit dissatisfied with how he'd expressed himself at a key point near the end of our session. Later, he reflected on what bothered him and was able to reword the point. He then went to the trouble to send me a long text with his clarification. I texted back my appreciation and said that we'd discuss it in our next get-together. When that next time rolled around, I completely forgot about his text; but that didn't become apparent until we returned

---

12. Lovelace, *Dynamics*, 88.

THREE QUESTIONS FOR SPIRITUAL CONVERSATIONS

to a theme from the previous session. That led to his mentioning the text, and I said, "Oh yeah, that's right! You sent that text!" In my chagrined realization that I'd forgotten, I simply stated the obvious! Then I tried to find the text in my phone and couldn't. He smoothed it over by quickly finding it in *his* phone and reading it to me. We then moved on to discuss how he sometimes struggles to trust others, and he began talking about a disappointing work situation. As he talked about third parties at work, he kept using the pronoun "you," as in, "When I delegate something to you and you claim to care about the task, but the reality is you don't actually do it, then I just tend to take over and make it right, but it's costly to me." As I listened to the mounting "yous," I felt discomfort. I was tempted to think, "He's just using a generic 'you,' as we often do, to refer to third parties." But another part of me thought, "He's commenting on my forgetting about the 'task' he assigned me by sending his text." After about the fifth or sixth "you," I asked, "What was it like for you that I dropped the ball and forgot about your text, and not only that, I couldn't find it?" He paused and put his hand over his face, hiding the emotions that transformed it. Dropping his hand back to his lap, he looked right at me and said, "Just now, when you called attention to your dropping the ball, I felt cared for. I felt known. I felt relief. But before you admitted your mistake, when I found my text in my phone and read it to you, I was just doing what I always do: giving up on being known, fixing it myself, and just dying to anything my heart might want from others. And that was beginning to feel terrible." I apologized, saying that he had, indeed, given me an important task in sending me his text, and I had failed him. Our discussion became warm and animated as contrasted with the tightly controlled sentences he'd given me before I admitted my blunder.

What is going on inside the other? He or she is wondering, "Will I end up in the same story with this helper as I have with others?" In other words, will the other find in the helper at least some hints of a new story, *or* will he or she end up in the same contest with the helper as has been endured in previous relationships? When I called attention to my failure, the other's heart was pierced by hope. Could this mean, he asked himself, I could now be in a story where my heart really matters? The hope here is that his heart could move from a thing contended *against* to its being contended *for*. When we contend against one another, we foster mere arrangements. When we contend for one another, we sow the seeds of actual relationships.

What is required to move from arrangements to relationships? First, it means repenting of the goal hidden with our forming mere arrangements. The goal is that we focus on getting and having without *looking* as though getting and having is the order of the day. The big lie that God has a hidden agenda comes with the powerful implication that if we can't trust the Creator, we certainly can't trust the creature. This mistrust leads to a drive to accumulate: with a subtle checklist of the outcomes we must have, we thrust toward amassing them. This energy pulses within the arrangements we impose on each other. Repenting of the goal of arrangements requires a deeper repentance, that of turning from the lie about God's character.

Second, moving from arrangements to relationships means caring how the other is faring in the war zone, the heart. How is he or she getting on in throwing off the distortions of the kingdom of darkness? Or not? How is he or she getting on in resolving the contention with others? Or not? How is he or she getting on in healing the contention with himself or herself? Or not? The helper's motive, then, is to move away from self-concern and to arrive where the other actually *is*, no matter *where* that is. To the degree that the helper has not personally dealt with "truth in the innermost being," the journey toward the other will be overwhelming.

WHAT IS GOD UP TO?

Beneath this second question is the idea that God is purposeful and involved in the lives of humans. Psalm 121:2 states: "My help comes from the Lord, / Who made heaven and earth." Commenting on this verse, Weiser says:

> For from this it appears that the concept of creation is not limited to the thought of the creation of the universe as an act of God that happened but once. The activity

of the Creator extends beyond the creation of the world;
the Creator-God is not dormant, but continues to act; he
is for ever the *living* God. Thus creation in the biblical
sense is comprehended as the living power of God which
continues to operate and is constantly creative. The . . .
biblical idea of creation . . . entails that creation and history, the past and the present, are welded into a unity,
and it imparts to the latter the significance of an actual
event which affects the life of the individual.[13]

How, then, does God's imbrication in history affect the human creature? Most crucially, in the one event of the incarnation, teaching, death, resurrection, and ascension of Jesus Christ. I use the term "event" to show that these five occasions are components of the massive intervention of God in the sending of God's "only begotten Son" (John 3:16), an explosion of "grace and truth" (John 1:14) that radiates backward into the life of, say, a Moses and forward into every human now living. The words "every human" are not meant to leave out Christ's effects on the rest of creation (animals, trees, mountains, and so on) but only to make the point that helpers sit across from fellow humans whose lives are probed by the radiance of Christ. Whatever God is up to, it will involve opening hearts to the implications of Christocentric radiance. Such an opening will always entail seeing the faint outlines of doorways a fellow struggler might present through his or her initial concerns.

Beyond the Initial Topics

Going back to the meeting where the man discussed his struggle to trust others to care and do a good job on tasks he has delegated, we see that as he painstakingly described a work situation, he wasn't really focusing there. As he repeated the word "you," I began to see a doorway. What's more, I began to sense that behind the door were some issues in his relationship with me. If I had ignored the door, being content to give him advice on how to handle the work frustrations, I'd have been adding insult to injury. First, I forgot about his

13. Weiser, *Psalms*, 748.

text and couldn't even find it; second, I'd have been hiding that empathic lapse within a dead zone of advice giving. He'd have heard the message "I am more alone than ever, and these patterns where both myself and others collaborate to bypass my heart will go on forever." Staying with the initial topics may promote hopelessness.

The metaphor of hidden doorways implies that often a code dots-and-dashes its way through our words and actions. A helper who ignores those doorways can't be said to be having spiritual conversations. Most of our behaving and speaking insinuates deeper things. I like "insinuate," because it contains the idea of sinuousness, which pictures well the fact that—winding in and out of our interactions—codes and hints of deeper meaning appear and disappear. Locking onto the surface import of what another says or does guarantees a comfortable, sterile superficiality and pushes away the discomfiting joy of entering doorways that reveal paths to the heart.

Beyond Initial Topics into What?

What *is* God up to, given the coming of Christ? God labors at restoring the ruins, the tumbled-down and destroyed God-human friendship. We're in the sad state of having lost our best, trustworthy, and eternal friend. And we have lost him by leaving him in a strange combination of sorrow and rebellion, nostalgia and aggression, wistfulness and distrustful distancing. We *are* conflicted! The conflict runs all the way through us, and we cannot solve it. We can only live in the ruins and labor to live out a sad, compensatory narrative: the ruins are bleak, but we can bootstrap our way into ruin repair (so we think). Out of our self-effort, a new Tower of Babel might rise, poking at least a few stories above the rubble. We can even call the leftover rubble an "architectural skirt." A cinder-block Babel with a rubble tutu! And that's the good life! This is otherwise known as decorating the pigsty. I don't intend the hard language here in a denigrating way. Rather, the tone is meant to be sobering. These conflicts are our *real* situation in life. In the second book of this series, *Cleanup*, I included a diagram that applies here, too:

THREE QUESTIONS FOR SPIRITUAL CONVERSATIONS

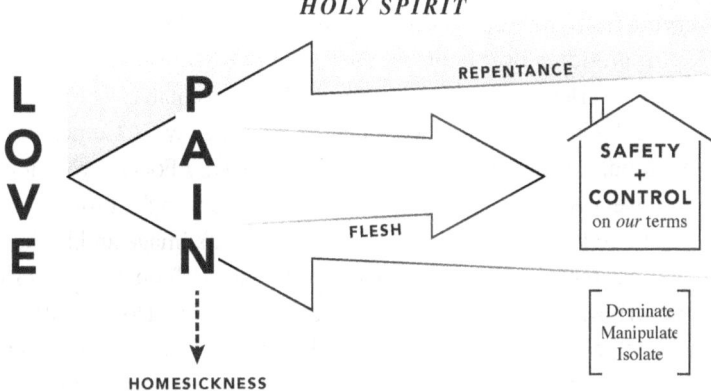

The house icon at the end of the flesh-driven arrow conveys the seriousness of the Babel metaphor. The "house" implies a *habitat* made of *habits* of pseudo-relating whose real agenda is to instigate arrangements through which others are managed, neutralized, ignored, or observed for categorization. These relational habits settle into deep routines of protective practices that run through our lives like marbling through beef. They look as if they're part of the "meat" but are really more like viruses that dis-ease our relationships, reshaping them into barren habit-dances that resemble two monsters having a tea party. It all looks polite and decorous, yet something monstrous is going on: an opportunity to talk about the real story of humans living on a fallen planet simply dies under the weight of compulsive prattle, of what Heidegger calls "idle talk."[14] What actually dies is reality. While the routine small talk at the tea party seems solid enough in its bluff pretense, it walks on the side of unreality, which is perilously close to the chaos depicted in Gen 1:2: "And the earth was formless and void, and darkness was over the surface of the deep." This chaos is what Barth calls "nothingness," the satanic bid to reduce all of creation to a shuddering naught. It is the wrong that opposes God and seeks to impose its no over all of God's handiwork.[15]

---

14. Heidegger, *Being and Time*, 212–13.
15. Barth, *Doctrine of Reconciliation*, 178.

UNSTUCK

And yet there is, at the top of the diagram, like Lady Wisdom crying from the "tops of the heights of the city" (Prov 9:3), the Holy Spirit presiding over hope. As the "Spirit of Christ" (Rom 8:9, 1 Pet 1:11), he cries along with Wisdom, "'Whoever is naive, let him turn in here!' / To him who lacks understanding she says, / 'Come, eat of my food, / And drink of the wine I have mixed. / Forsake your folly and live, / And proceed in the way of understanding'" (Prov 9:4–6). The hope is that, because we are made in God's image and because God has sent the Holy Spirit (God from God) to "convict the world concerning sin, and righteousness, and judgment" (John 16:8), we will actually betray ourselves in code. For example, the consistent choice of "you" in the man's report of his disappointments at work was code for "I am really disappointed, Steve, in your negligence. I don't feel cared for." Through listening well (to be discussed in chapter 2), helpers can learn to discern the hints of hidden doorways. These codes form an archipelago of narrative glimpsed through a fog. Blurred by the routines of the habit-dance, the crucial narrative of struggle in a fallen world threatens to disappear, like Atlantis. Yet, the Holy Spirit, passionate for truth, hides below the hiddenness, working to make it buoyant. Tiny pontoons of truth appear briefly in these coded forms. The Spirit reveals narrative threads that may become the bases for spiritual conversations. In those all-too-rare conversations, this is what God is up to. One hope of this book is to engender more of such Spirit-led conversations—i.e., spiritual conversations. To align with what God is up to, we must learn to see more clearly, and this advances us to our next question.

HOW DOES ONE SEE CLEARLY?

We have reflected on the following questions: (1) What is going on inside (the helper and the other)? (2) What is God up to? Our third question echoes the fact that in the fog of routine living, our powers of discernment weaken. When someone needs help, how do we see clearly in order to transform routine talk into spiritual conversation?

THREE QUESTIONS FOR SPIRITUAL CONVERSATIONS

Life as Unmanageable

The helper's vantage point is crucial. Assuming that life in a fallen world is manageable creates a sight line oriented around regarding the other's maladjusted thinking and behavior simply as surface problems that need fixing. On the other hand, if one assumes that a fallen world is by nature unmanageable, the sight line shifts to view behavior and thinking as opportunities for exploring.

But what do I mean by "unmanageable"? I *don't* mean that life is inherently unplannable; nor do I mean that we should take a slipshod, careless approach to our journey. Instead, I mean that there are simply too many contingencies in life, too many didn't-see-that-coming developments, to pretend that life can be wrestled into a smoothly running mechanism. As one commentator puts it, the world "has an obstinate shape which we cannot iron out to our liking (which therefore . . . has a certain built-in resistance, mercifully enough, to us as planners and standardizers); for 'who can make straight what he has made crooked?' ([Eccl] 7:13)."[16] Because our flesh urges us to establish control, we habitually deny life's unmanageability. The helper must work toward *planning* to do the other person good rather than *managing* the other in order to keep the helper comfortable. If we go where people really are, we will often have that out-of-control feeling; and that's a matter not for doubling down on control but for prayer. And prayer must focus on two issues: self-examination (again, "What is going on in me as I seek to help?") and wisdom ("What does it mean, in this discomfort, to wait patiently for the Lord's perspective for this person?").

Working hard to stay in control will narrow our perspective by limiting us to the question "Am I comfortable with what is happening in me or in the other? And, if not, how can I manage things so that I'm back in my comfort zone?" If we *accept* the unmanageability of life, we *expand* our capacity to come alongside others. We can relax by letting go of our hidden agenda that things turn out comfortably for us, and relaxing—simply because we're more open—helps us see more clearly.

---

16. Kidner, *A Time to Mourn*, 15.

UNSTUCK

The Flesh is a Fogbank

Refer again to the "house" icon at the end of the flesh arrow on page 15. To the left of the house, an arrow rushes toward it, driven by the flesh's lie that pain is the enemy and must be minimized, managed, and controlled. This urgency harasses us toward our version of safety and control, hounding us to make sure we have the outcomes that constitute the same. Urged, harassed, and hounded, we live sped-up lives, as if we're the fox and pain is the pack of baying hounds. The deep, driving force of this survival engine dictates that we'll fail to see ourselves or others clearly. In Gal 5:13, we learn, "For you were called to freedom, brethren; only do not turn your freedom into an opportunity for the flesh." The word translated "opportunity" is *aphormē*, which means "*a starting point*; in war, *a base of operations*."[17] Paul uses a metaphor: the flesh is an armed band looking for a tactical advantage, seeking a likely jumping-off point from which to hit the enemy with concentrated force. He regards the flesh both as a tactician and a sneaky opportunist. Our flesh patterns, then, don't announce themselves. Fair warning is not the flesh's nature, which is why Paul tells us elsewhere to put it to death (Rom 8:13). Otherwise, we are flying blind. The result of this blindness is the following:

> Men may have . . . corruptions, which, either by their natural constitution or education, and other prejudices, have got deep rooting and strength in them. This is to be found out by him who would not enter into temptation. Unless he know it, unless his eyes be always on it, unless he observes its actings, motions, advantages, it will continually be entangling and ensnaring of him . . . . Be acquainted, then, with thine own heart: though it be deep, search it; though it be dark, inquire into it; though it give all its distempers other names than what are their due, believe it not. Were not men utter strangers to themselves . . . did they not strive . . . to justify . . . the evils of their hearts . . . it were impossible that they should all

---

17. Abbott-Smith, *Greek Lexicon*, 72; italics in the original.

their days hang in the same briers without attempt for deliverance.[18]

The helper will not see clearly while hanging "in the same briers" in which the opportunistic flesh has habitually entangled him or her. Paul, however, walks in hope of our being disentangled as he leads us along God's way in Rom 8:13, writing, "If *by the Spirit* you are putting to death the deeds of the body . . ." (italics mine). Only the Holy Spirit is a match, and more than a match, for our below-the-radar fleshly tactics. The Spirit of Christ (another term for the Holy Spirit) works to bring to mind the subtle habits that drive us unreflectively toward our idiosyncratic versions of safety and control. No helper can see those habits in another who has not soberly faced them in his or her own self. A key to seeing well, then, is the quality of our own repentance.

The presence of the indwelling Spirit (dwelling more deeply than indwelling sin) raises the issue of God as Trinity and introduces us to yet another way to see more clearly.

The Trinity as Relational Invitation

Most Christians have become used to thinking of God as one God existing as a unity yet in three persons. This is accurate, but it's usually about where we stop. The Trinity devolves, then, into a head-scratching datum that is vaguely profound but seeming to be without import for the question of how actually we are to live. In regarding the Trinity as an interesting fact, we miss vast opportunities to see more clearly. Why?

The Father has personhood, and he has always—eternally— been willing to share it with another. This other is the Son, Jesus Christ, who has *always* been begotten by the Father; that is, given being, but not by creation (the Son is not a created being but is coequal with the Father in all things except the capacity to beget). Within the gift of Jesus' eternal being comes the quality of personhood. In God, the nature of personhood *is* to be in relationship:

---

18. Owen, "Of Temptation," 132.

"Father is the name of a relation: Father of the Son."[19] This begetting, then, is the eternal sharing of personhood with another so that the Son may share love with the Father. It is the nature of God to be in relationship—first, within himself in the mutual love of Father and Son. This bond of love is the Holy Spirit, the one who proceeds from the Father and Son in the form of love borne back and forth, a coalescence in that love that has always been.[20] This "coalescence," the Holy Spirit, is also personal. The unfettered mutuality among the three within the one creates a model for what it is to be human. The flesh, on the other hand, creates a model for what it is to be *in*human as its drive to win at securing outcomes creates an anxious striving for scarce goods in an atmosphere of insecurity.

On the other hand, "Because God is an eternal community of three persons in perpetual perichoretic relating, to bear His image means that we have the capacity and calling to relate similarly to each other."[21] Reflecting a similar Trinitarian emphasis, Lacugna says, "Entering into the life of God means entering in the deepest way possible into the economy, into the life of Jesus Christ, into the life of the Spirit, into the life of others. . . . Entering divine life is therefore impossible unless we also enter into a life of love and communion with others."[22] Moltmann puts the impact of Trinitarian thought this way: "The New Testament talks about God by proclaiming in narrative the relationships of the Father, the Son and the Spirit, which are relationships of fellowship and are open to the world."[23] How do these Trinitarian discoveries affect our seeing? They open our eyes to see that others are not problems to be solved but relationships to be entered and developed. Even when others present specific problems to be solved, on a deeper level (and perhaps not consciously), they are asking to be accompanied. "Will you keep me company in my struggle?"—this is their longing.

---

19. Lacugna, *God for Us*, 390.
20. Congar, *I Believe*, 88.
21. Crabb, "School of Spiritual Direction," 111; all caps and italics removed.
22. Lacugna, *God for Us*, 382; italics removed.
23. Moltmann, *Trinity and the Kingdom*, 64; italics removed.

THREE QUESTIONS FOR SPIRITUAL CONVERSATIONS

Again, this is a way of seeing and thus a way to look beyond the immediate, presenting persona of the other. Rarely will others simply begin by presenting a completely naked look at their core conflicts. In fact, they often don't know clearly what those conflicts are. The helper's Trinitarian-based willingness to see *through* the outward layer of social acceptability, defensiveness, and external routines of relating will help the helper assess what God might be up to in the other's soul. The only way helpers will be able to see others *through* their journeys is to see *through* the outward proprieties that conceal the real issues. And this *seeing through* is a deeply Trinitarian concept, based as it is on the nothing-hidden, mutual openness of Father, Son, and Spirit to one another.

Dual Citizenship

In Phil 3:20–21, Paul says, "For our citizenship is in heaven, from which also we eagerly wait for a Savior, the Lord Jesus Christ." One commentator renders the opening phrase as follows: "We are a colony of Heaven."[24] Am I, the writer, a citizen of the United States? Yes. Does this citizenship entail serious responsibilities? Yes. Is it my primary citizenship? No. According to Paul's understanding, the believer in Christ has a higher loyalty that makes relative any earthly loyalty. A central question for the Christian follows: In the midst of my short life on earth, am I living as an outpost of God's kingdom?

Among other things, this question sets us up to understand the disorienting theme of Heb 11:13–16:

> All these [Old Testament people of faith] died in faith, without receiving the promises, but having seen them and having welcomed them from a distance, and having confessed that they were strangers and exiles on the earth. For those who say such things make it clear that they are seeking a country of their own. And indeed if they had been thinking of that country from which they went out [their literal home country], they would have

---

24. Abott-Smith, *Greek Lexicon*, 371.

had opportunity to return. But as it is, they desire a better country, that is a heavenly one. Therefore God is not ashamed to be called their God; for He has prepared a city for them.

I call the theme of this passage "disorienting," because it announces that a mark of the Christian is that the conditions that prevail in earthly life create in him or her a sense of exile. The powerful undertow of social and cultural inputs that believers daily experience seeks to seduce us into assuming, "My one shot at the good life lies in how I play my cards within my life on this planet." If we're not careful, we end up playing as skillfully as possible the hand we're dealt, losing sight of our citizenship in heaven and of our longing for the "better country" that God has in store through his creating "new heavens and a new earth" (2 Pet 3:13) when Jesus returns to restore all things.

The theme of dual citizenship with an emphasis on heavenly citizenship as our priority helps us see by proposing that we regard everything *sub specie aeternitatis* ("under the form of eternity"). As helpers who seek to foment spiritual conversations, we're responsible for seeing through the big-picture lens of eternity. It's as if, having seen dozens of major-league baseball games, we're sitting down with a T-ball player and beginning to sketch out "how it can be." Of course, the analogy breaks down when we realize that T-ball players are five or six years old, but you get the idea. We're aware of a big vision and constantly wonder what it looks like to translate that vision on behalf of our fellow pilgrims, who are our fellow strugglers.

Seeing from an eternal, Trinitarian sight line also helps us relieve the other from artificial pressure to "win" the game of accumulating enough culturally approved outcomes to wear the "I found the good life" merit badge. Many internal conflicts derive from a sense of falling short of cultural ideals that may or may not be warranted by the citizenship-in-heaven ethos. Others will sit across from the helper, burdened by shame owing to performance pressure (just to use one example of shame) from the massive advertising forces that nudge, cajole, wheedle, and batter one through each day ("Drive this car"; "Eat that food"; "Dress for this

THREE QUESTIONS FOR SPIRITUAL CONVERSATIONS

look"; "Have the body for that look"; "Own this device"; "Listen to that music"). Citizens of heaven learn to sense the falsity within these frantic creations of artificial value. Helpers who are aware of a dual citizenship will come alongside to take the pressure off the gasping, exhausted struggler.

Surfacing Pain in Words

Helpers bring heaven to earth in their willingness to make a space for pain; first, for the feeling of pain, and then for its expression in words. Brueggemann, writing in a pastoral vein, says, "I suggest that congregations must be, in intentional ways, *communities of honest sadness*, naming the losses . . . . The community of sadness has as its work the countering of the 'culture of denial' which continues to imagine that it [life] is as it was, even when our experience tells otherwise."[25] He goes on elsewhere, "Everything is said, and God is known to be strong enough and willing enough to hear."[26] Denial of pain means the impossibility of working through problems. The importance of surfacing pain in honest, accurate words provides the helper a sight line along which he or she values struggles as messengers. If pain can't speak, then life-changing messages may die inside the speechlessness. The helper, aided by the stance of "everything under the form of eternity," is not willing that the messages remain unborn. Like a midwife, he or she helps them come to light.

Imagine the following scenario: as an oldest son grows up, it becomes clear he is endowed with tremendous academic and athletic gifts, the latter giving him clear potential for a career in a professional sport. Throwing all his energy into athletics, he underperforms academically in college. Rising in the minor leagues with a glowing future, he blows out a knee. In his day, sports medicine hadn't nearly the restorational power of today. His career is over. The ship of grad school has sailed owing to his mediocre academic showing. So, through a friend of a friend (no websites in that era), he finds a job selling paper. After twenty years as a salesman, he

---

25. Brueggemann, *Cadences of Home*, 4.
26. Brueggemann, *Psalms*, 58.

begins, seemingly out of nowhere, to struggle with mental illness. At the core of it is suppressed pain of two sorts: (1) that of living in a fallen world, far from Eden; and (2) the focused pain in the shame of squandering his gifts. We can, and I think should, add a third pain, that of the second pain inflaming the first, escalating it from a dull ache to a searing burn in the soul: "How can I survive living so far from home? The lonely pain of exile is unbearable! I've worked so hard to keep it under wraps, but now it's like holding a beach ball under water." None of these words were ever spoken.

Why are words so important in relationship to pain? One answer is born from the fact that Jesus Christ is God's "Word" to the world. The magisterial sentences in John's Gospel sketch out for us a Word-drenched world: "In the beginning was the Word, and the Word was with God, and the Word was God.... And the Word became flesh, and dwelt among us" (John 1:1, 14). A similar thought emerges in Heb 1:1–2: "God, after He spoke long ago to the fathers in the prophets in many portions and in many ways, in these last days has spoken to us in His Son, whom He appointed heir of all things, through whom also He made the world." Jesus is God speaking to the world. When God saw the plight of the world, God sent a living Word to encounter our crisis through the luminous arrival of speech wrapped in a living person. This livingness gives the speech an eventfulness that conveys a dawning, an eventful collision with a stagnant world that seeks to shake it awake.

One implication is that humans are people with a deep penchant for words. We find words attractive; we like them, because through them we can find "likenings"—that is, analogies that shed light on merely brute experience. It's no surprise, then, that when the Word comes, he often teaches through "likenings"—i.e., he likens a familiar thing to an unfamiliar, shedding light on the latter: "The kingdom of heaven is like . . ." We know these "likenings" as his parables.

Suppose the man who blew out his knee had a helper who provided a space where eventually he finds clarifying words:

> It's as if I'm frantically throwing things at the wall to see what will stick. School didn't stick. Sports didn't stick.

THREE QUESTIONS FOR SPIRITUAL CONVERSATIONS

> Now my sales are slipping. Younger guys are coming in with all this energy. I have to work harder than ever. I throw more and more stuff at the wall, but it all slides off. Then I look across at my younger brother—I always thought of him as slower, less talented. But these days, everything *he* throws at the wall sticks like crazy glue! I can't stand it! It's like watching a dancing bear win an award in ballet! It's not fair! Life doesn't make any sense!

Note the words "as if" in his first sentence. With this power of likening, he has much more of a chance to see how he's interpreting the journey of his life. As he surfaces his pain in words, he can recognize the story he's telling himself. The new dawning may lead to questions that bring more depth of understanding; for example, what may have happened early in his life that put him under intense pressure to succeed? And how did he learn to define success in his particular way? Only through *fresh words that name the pain* can he understand the story that confines him. And only then might a counter-story, *also in fresh words*, become available in a spiritual conversation between two who have deeply connected in relationship.

The "Social Imaginary"

The concept of a "social imaginary" refines the idea of a worldview. More than a way of looking at the world, a social imaginary is the sum of (1) what a society imagines to be normative and (2) how its norms might create new possibilities. In other words, societies form collective pictures that convey "This is the kind of world at which we're aiming." A social imaginary, then, is an imaginative act of creation in the aggregate. It gives the society in which it operates a sense of coherence, much as a set of rules organizes a game.[27] As Taylor puts it, "[T]he social imaginary is that common understanding that makes possible common practices and a widely shared sense of legitimacy."[28]

---

27. Earle, "Social Imaginary," paras. 1–2.
28. Taylor, *Modern Social Imaginaries*, 23.

UNSTUCK

Social philosopher Samantha Earle has concluded, after extensive research, that the center of the social imaginary for Western society is a sense of entitlement.[29] If we grant the truth of her conclusion, we might conclude that it would be wise for helpers to include it as a line of sight in spiritual conversations. A society influenced by an upwelling of entitlement would induce a majority to lay claim to a finite supply of goods. Advertising, along with the social posturing of leisure and affluence, would create an urgency not to lose ground in the race for asserting titular legitimacy to this good or that. Anxiety about claim jumping would permeate the social atmosphere.

In such a social imaginary, many who seek help through spiritual conversations may need permission to explore the performance pressure generated by the norms of an entitled society. Further, helpers won't be able to use this line of sight unless we face our own embeddedness in the social imaginary. But how do we do this? Isn't this like asking a fish to figure out that it's wet? This task *is* difficult, but it's not impossible; for the kingdom of God provides a transcendent "social imaginary," as Jesus teaches deeply countercultural values: "And if any one wants to sue you, and take your shirt, let him have your coat also" (Matt 5:40). The Lord's teaching urges his followers radically to relinquish their titles to worldly goods. Part of the reason his new norm is so uncomfortable is that it flies in the face of the Western social imaginary. At the same time, it offers a sufficiently shocking disruption such that it invites us to step outside our modern/postmodern rules for conducting life. That is, it beckons the helper to that new line of sight that can inform spiritual conversations. Newly liberated from the Western social imaginary, they can be like cool water offered to any who are weary from anxious striving in an exhausting rush for "the good life."

---

29. Earle, "Social Imaginary," para. 26.

CHAPTER 2

Listening

We have been exploring three questions: What is going on inside both the helper and the other? What is God up to? How may we see more clearly? Along the way, the reader may be asking, "How do we gather enough information even to begin answering these questions?" Simple answer: listening. True listening reflects a commitment to go where the other truly *is*. From a distance, a shepherd cannot help a sheep stuck in a mudhole. The shepherd simply has to move forward and get in the mudhole to do any good. Real listening takes us into the stuck, messy lostness of others. As you can see from the repetitions so far, this commitment to show up where the other actually struggles is essential to spiritual conversation.

THE NATURE OF LISTENING

What is listening? Listening is a whole-person engagement to receive comprehensively the signals another communicates. As such, it closes the distance, engaging the other at all the points of struggle, frustration, and blocked hope. One therapist puts it this way: "Therefore, like a blind man, I try to listen for the different kinds of echo that are reflected back to me from each step that I take in a session."[1] The metaphor of the blind man and the echo richly enables an understanding of listening as eschewing a supposed pre-understanding of what the other seeks to convey. This disciplined forgoing of a supposed foreknowledge increases our capacity to pick up "echoes"—that is, to reap what opens up from the other when we don't foreclose on it because of our own need for certainty. Another helper says, "You haven't really heard someone until you're in touch with the terror of your own inadequacy."[2] Why would truly hearing another bring such fear? Because at the core of every soul is a battle with nonbeing, and that is the same battle in which the helper is engulfed. What I mean by the "battle with nonbeing" is best captured by Jesus' saying that "the thief comes only to steal, and kill, and destroy" (John 10:10). The three strong verbs here point to an intelligence whose corrupt nature aims at the undoing of creaturely existence. When we get close to the core fears in others, we and they approach a dark frequency that announces the campaign to pull us into pieces. If the other is transparent and we are attuned to him or her, we will suffer through surges of discomfort. As will the other. If both remain faithful to the Spirit's longing to foster growth, the suffering stands a solid chance of bearing fruit.

Listening is absorbing all (or as close to all as possible) the signals the other communicates. The listener is like a sponge absorbing what pours out of the other. And this outpouring is not simple. It combines both the expression of pain and of "unconscious relational style."[3] The latter is the sum of embedded tactics of safety and control, of which the other is largely unaware. Another therapist describes these tactics by the term "process"—that is, the other's unwitting setting up of an "interpersonal scenario."[4] Listening, then, seeks to understand this enacted scenario and the roots and function of it. But while taking in the outlines of this scenario, the listener must never lose sight of (1) his/her *own* tendencies to

1. Casement, *Learning from the Patient*, 54.
2. Crabb, "School of Spiritual Direction." Here, the author transcribed Dr. Crabb's words from the lecture verbatim.
3. Crabb, "School of Spiritual Direction." Here, the author transcribed Dr. Crabb's words from the lecture verbatim.
4. Strupp and Binder, *Psychotherapy*, 90–91.

LISTENING

enact process, (2) the other's pain, or (3) the relationship between the current self of the other and his/her "eschatological identity."[5] All these must dance together within and between helper and other in that "transitional space" that Gerkin describes: "The work/play of the counseling hermeneutical circle may thus be seen as being undertaken in the hope and expectation of opening up transitional space within which new and potentially transforming truths, part imaginative interpretation and part new acknowledgment of reality, may come forcefully into play."[6] While helpers don't do counseling per se, they follow Gerkin's model of circling through the stations of the other's pain and scenario crafting, combined with awareness of the helper's own vulnerability to pain and unwitting scripting of the other. The helper is constantly listening within and without. The "transitional space" can be thought of as a free space where spiritual conversations progressively abstain from the scripting of one another that is part and parcel of scenario crafting.

THE FOCAL POINTS OF LISTENING

Listening is an act of caring and, as such, takes the content of the other's speech seriously. It does not, then, preoccupy itself with what words to say next, for it values the actual words of the other, treating them as bearing the freight of meaning. At the same time, the listener remains aware that words can sometimes *hide* meaning. For example, the other says, "I just say what I feel, and I don't care what others think." Is that literally true, or is it a feint to distract from how vulnerable to opinion he or she really is? Is this a bare statement of fact, or is it part of an interpersonal scenario where mere assertion bids to count as reality while another truth lurks beneath? It will take a lot of listening to create the transitional space where, free of scripting, the other might reveal the pain of struggling with the weight of outside opinion.

This continuing theme of interpersonal scenario on one side and the hope of non-scripted transitional space on the other makes

---

5. Gerkin, *Living Human Document*, 156.
6. Gerkin, *Living Human Document*, 153–54.

listening a dramatic act, part of the unfolding of a story whose outcome remains in suspense. Is the listener willing to endure discomfort and to engage patiently such that defensive scripting becomes less important on both sides? Or will the new story that waits to be born collapse under old defenses and fears?

In order to increase the data available to the helper, he or she must engage with nonverbal aspects of communication: tone of voice, vocal cadence, eye contact (or lack of it), posture, gesture (or lack of it), and facial expression. By "vocal cadence," I mean the pace of speech and whether it creates the impression of being uninterruptible. One who strings sentences together like tightly linked, swift railroad cars may be using speech to dominate the relationship *or* may ache with a desperate need to be heard. Either way, the listener is alerted to be curious about the interpersonal scenario.

Another important focal point of listening is to tune in to what *isn't* said. If the other speaks about important relationships for half an hour without, say, mentioning anything about his or her father, the father absent in speech may be very present in a complex way in the other's story. This conclusion can't be assumed, but tuning in to its possibility *may* reveal a doorway. Such attunement to lacunae requires the listener's not being preoccupied with extraneous issues such as looking competent or needing to be helpful. If such issues *are* in the foreground for the helper, that probably indicates the presence of the helper's own interpersonal scenario. He or she may be treating the other as an opportunity to feel effective. If so, the interaction will be stiff with prescriptive talk, reflecting the prescripting under which the helper labors. In that case, the helper must listen internally, asking, "What is at stake for me such that I am scripting both myself and the other?"

As I write this, it dawns on me that just yesterday, I sat with an older man who drove up in a gigantic, uber-expensive truck, wore a tight T-shirt over a muscular torso, and spoke with a confident tone throughout. We covered a lot of ground on the level of content, but I missed an opportunity to put together enough data to realize what I was presented with: powerful truck, powerful body, powerful voice. I see now that I will need to assist him to see why power is such a crucial theme for him. *And* I must ask myself, "What was at stake

LISTENING

for me that I missed that opportunity? What is my history with power that may have influenced me in that conversation? Could it have been more of a *spiritual* conversation had I not unconsciously bracketed out some of the data?"

Let's suppose I *had* expressed curiosity about his preoccupation with power. And suppose my curiosity provoked defensiveness, his speech becoming louder and more rapid, his gestures becoming more pronounced, his eyes narrowing. That kind of change in intensity is a *shift*, and such sudden variations always convey that important issues are stirring inside the other. The helper listens to the shift and wonders, "What is this defensiveness protecting?"

Another way to think about shifts is to assume that they're related to a *backstory*. A backstory is a narrative that has been shoved into the background. The story (which may or may not be conscious to the other) carries an emotional charge, and when conversing approaches it, enough of the charge may surface to cause the observable shift.

Finally, outright changes of subject are a subtype of shift. Just as with the more obvious emotional shift, the change of subject reflects a backstory from which it is time to flee. Again, the backstory may not be conscious. I am not speaking about open deception here but about a vague discomfort in the other that calls for evasion. A deep cry of the heart has been denied, and spiritual conversations may "stray" near the pain pocket. We'll have more say about backstory in our next chapter.

LISTENING TO GOD

A tricky subject, this one. I am not suggesting that direct revelation from God may surge into the consciousness of the helper as it did the prophets and apostles. I believe the canon of Scripture is closed and that such revelation, normative for the whole people of God, has ceased until Christ returns. On the other hand, the Holy Spirit indwells the believing helper. In other words, the helper has a Helper.

UNSTUCK

An exploration of Jas 4:5 may help us understand the agenda of the divine Helper: "Or do you think that the Scripture speaks to no purpose: 'He jealously desires the Spirit which He has made to dwell in us?'" The writer, James, the half brother of Jesus, addresses Christians here. He sees believers in Christ as having been given the Holy Spirit to dwell inside them (see, for comparison, 1 Cor 6:19). James depicts God, the giver of the Spirit, as longing—even to the point of jealousy—for this same Spirit that dwells within us. In what sense, then, does God long for the Spirit in us? In light of the previous context, which speaks of "quarrels and conflicts among you" (Jas 4:1), of "lusts" and even "murder" (Jas 4:2, although the latter could be meant figuratively), it seems proper to interpret Jas 4:5 as God's intense yearning to see evidence of the Holy Spirit filling the lives of believers, transforming us into those who look "intently at the perfect law, the law of liberty," abiding by it, "not having become a forgetful hearer but an effectual doer" (Jas 1:25). Such "effectual doer[s]" are not, to say the least, filled with quarrels and lust and murder.

What might this passage imply regarding the helper's listening to God? Given that God is "jealous" for glimpses of the Holy Spirit's work in his children, might we say that the helper stays attuned to what the Lord might long to convey to the other along the lines of the Spirit's gaining more freedom to fill the other's life? Another way of expressing this might be that the helper longs to see what God longs to see: the other coming alive with the life of God's kingdom.

Assuming that both ways of expressing the helper's attunement are correct, would it not make sense, then, that the helper disciplines him- or herself to gain an understanding of the story in which the other seems to be entangled? Earlier, we concluded that the human heart is a place of war. Now, we may add that one dimension of the conflict is that of opposing stories contending for the heart. The theme of clashing stories takes us to our next chapter.

CHAPTER 3

The Storied Self

Here, we tackle question four, which we left hanging near the beginning of chapter 1: How might the idea of story help us explore further what is going on inside, what God is up to, and how we may see more clearly? We find an avenue into this question through the doorway of contemporary psychotherapy.

A respected form of people helping these days is known as Acceptance and Commitment Therapy.[1] One of its goals is to invite the sufferer to shift from a stance called "self-as-*content*" to that of "self-as-*context*." The idea is that the self-as-content view sees the self as being fused with the content of whatever the person is feeling or thinking. In other words, "What I am thinking/feeling *is* who I am at the moment." The shift to "self-as-context" promotes the idea that the person may, indeed, be thinking or feeling x, but the person is the *context* for that thinking. That is, the individual contains and is larger than whatever thinking is going on and can step aside from the thinking, the feelings. "I am thinking x, but I can detach from x and shift my focus elsewhere. That shift may (or may not) include thinking *about* what I'm thinking. That might be an option, or I may think in a whole new direction. In any case, attention is portable."

---

1. Hayes and Smith, *Out of Your Mind*, 1.

UNSTUCK

As helpful as this shift may be, I'd prefer to go yet farther and use the concept of "self-as-*storied*." That is, the self is not only a context for thinking and feeling (which is true), but that same self exists *within* a context. The self not only contains but is contained. Contained by what? By the accumulated experiences in their tens of thousands that, instead of being disconnected like name after disconnected name in the old phone books, meld into a narrative of a life, a narrative that settles into the background and runs something like programming in a computer. I say "somewhat like," because an engineer can, with the right knowledge, probe into the computer and reveal the program's features. The helper in spiritual conversation is not like the engineer, and the internal story of the other is not clear as the program is clear. The helper doesn't wave a technological magic wand that produces the other's story. Rather, he or she elicits that story through engaged listening, treating it with respect and care. The story might be thought of as deposits of self-concept now sedimented deep in the soul and often poorly understood.[2] The other harbors a narrative self-understanding, yet the meanings of it may be little reflected upon as the action sequences of life move along like a carpet unrolling. As the cylinder of the carpet unrolls bit by bit, the patterns at the beginning may lose their clarity, casualties of a recency bias. Especially in Western culture, where it can be an important value to keep moving, the sediment of one's story may settle deeply within, remaining influential yet poorly grasped.

The strange place at which we've arrived so far in this chapter on stories is that we live in a context, that of those thousands of fork-in-the-road experiences that mark every life. This reality is part of the "self-as-storied." Yet, that same context has settled rather narrowly *inside* us as if poured through a funnel into a deep compartment. It's as though we live in a forest of life experiences that has somehow been hit by a shrink ray now to contract into a deep wood in some private province of the heart. The story that holds us is held deep inside. What contains us (the surrounding "forest" of life experiences) is also contained in deep files within the heart.

---

2. Ricoeur, *Time and Narrative*, 68.

THE STORIED SELF

The self, then, is storied by the experience-heavy quality of human life as the skein of experiences collects into a personal narrative. Yet, the settled-down-inside quality of the narrative means that it isn't yet a resource for self-understanding. It eludes insight. In spiritual conversations, this elusiveness has the effect of turning presenting issues into a screen that exacerbates this slippery quality of the life narrative. And yet, these concrete surface issues may also serve as a trailhead for spelunking into the self-as-storied in a deeper way. In this vein, "The solving of human problems is seen as fundamentally related to coming to grips with the deeper issues in the life of the soul. Human problems provide the *occasion* for the surfacing of these deeper issues."[3] The conscious problems the other brings to spiritual conversation, though not to be minimized, tend to reflect a self-as-content point of view. The helper hopes to invite the other to become discontent with self-as-content. The hope is that new discontentment will cause a helpful disruption that moves the other toward a self-as-storied stance. The move from "I have problems to be solved" to "I am a story being told and still yet to be told" gives the Holy Spirit much raw material for engendering "newness of life" (Rom 6:4). Emphasizing a problems-to-be-solved stance means remaining in an untold story. An untold story causes untold suffering, as we've seen through all four books in this series.

Here, I think back to the first book, *Stuck: How We Are Reverse Born Again*, remembering that story is a major part of why this whole book project was launched. That book essentially addresses how we get stuck in our stories. Throughout this series, we've been working toward the value of seeing life in a storied way. All too often, though, even when we approach story as a way of understanding our lives, we tend to think in a self-as-content sort of way, as we've seen. This is ironic, because as we step toward this idea of self-as-storied, we reduce the value of it by thinking in a self-as-content way about the fact that we're in a self-as-storied life! In other words, the *content* of our thinking about our story *is* the story (so we think). Maybe I could coin the phrase "*story*-as-content" to supplement the idea of self-as-content. "Story-as-content" implies

---

3. Gerkin, *Living Human Document*, 178; italics mine.

that my story is simply my conscious account of my life so far. The assumption here is that my knowledge of myself is exhaustive, an assumption that leaves out the crucial fact that humans tend to "suppress the truth in unrighteousness" (Rom 1:18). If we confine ourselves to the idea of story-as-content, then it takes on a repressive quality—this self-as-content stance toward story hides what's below, which is a life narrative (the shrunken wood) that, while hidden, exerts influence, yet does not yield much self-understanding. That understanding must come from a shift from story-as-content (my conscious story) to self-as-storied (probing below the screen of consciousness). This probe requires our not *stopping* with "storied" in the sense of a sedimented story that has been cooking along on some low level of programming. While it's important to delve into this sedimented story, spiritual conversations head toward realizing that God calls into our lives—calls about a larger, transcendent story that speaks to and works to alter the norms of the story in which we're programmed, the story that routinely runs in the depths, beyond our conscious knowing.

It's important to remember that the hidden, flesh-driven story (which is still part of self-as-storied) is self-deceptive. The result is that what one *purports* to be doing can be far from what one is *actually* doing. And one may not be aware (or want to be aware) that there's a gap between the espoused theory of what one's life story is and the actual theory in use.[4] In other words, one may claim to live an above-reproach story, but the story driving actual behaviors may be subtly self-interested. That gap between the two versions dictates that there will often be a troubled relationship between the claimed story and the truth. One of the scariest moments in my graduate counseling program was when a professor gave me the assignment to ask my wife, "What is it like to live with me? Be honest." Gulp. She *was* honest, and through her feedback, I learned sober truth concerning my *claims* about myself as opposed to what she actually *experienced* in her day-to-day relationship with me. What she experienced was the result of my below-awareness, flesh-driven story of seeking safety and control as I defined them.

---

4. Argyris, *Reasoning, Learning, and Action*, 85.

THE STORIED SELF

The idea of self-as-storied, then, invites us to open ourselves to the Holy Spirit's probe (in the above instance, through my professor) into the machinations of our suppressed, fleshly commitment to make life work on our own terms. Through my wife's honest, risky words, the Spirit closed the gap between my claims and the actual truth about myself. The truth brought conviction, and conviction overflowed into repentance. A spiritual conversation brought a spiritual renewal.

The idea of Spirit-led renewal brings us to the fact that self-as-storied relates to the eschatological self mentioned earlier. Since it's true that "it has not appeared as yet what we shall be. We know that, when He appears, we shall be like Him" (1 John 3:2), we anticipate a future self that is complete. In this life, the good life is that of seeking to grow to be more and more like Christ. Thus, we hope in this life increasingly to resemble our ultimate, future self. That goal helps us realize that right now, each of us is a formerly future self regarding who we were x years ago. That is, who I am now is the self toward which I was moving x years ago. The question is, was I then faithful to the self I am now? Or was I unfaithful (making foolish choices)? Am I now *not* the future self I might have been? Could I have learned more about what was driving me then so that I would now have been more the "me" God has always known I can be? When my wife was honest with me years ago, she was helping me become more faithful to my future self. If I had rebuffed her honesty, I'd be a much different self than I am at this point. Every spiritual conversation, then, has the potential to be a "mini-eschaton."

However, it's not just the future/eschatological self that connects with the self-as-storied but also the creation/covenant story that goes all the way back to creation and, really, before that; because in the mind of God, creation and covenant have been his eternal choice and will. The idea of the covenant is that God made an agreement within God's own self (and indirectly, with creation) to determine to be *for* creation and never to let it go, ever to pursue its good for God's glory and its own well-being. And that divine commitment is also a vital part of the transcendent story expressed in Rom 5:5: "And hope does not disappoint, because the love of God has been poured out in our hearts through the Holy

Spirit who was given to us." The outpouring of the Holy Spirit at Pentecost is part of the coming of Christ,[5] and whenever Christ comes, he brings a rereading of life. All we need do to confirm this is to remember what happened when the risen Christ met two disciples on the road to Emmaus. There, he opened the Old Testament to them, "and beginning with Moses and with all the prophets, He explained to them the things concerning Himself in all the Scriptures" (Luke 24:27). Jesus reread the story—having emerged, as it were, from its scrolls—turning around and giving it back its proper dimensions. A rereading of life indeed! A spiritual conversation of the first magnitude!

In spiritual conversations, as defined in this book, a tension emerges regarding plausibility and implausibility. When we think of the story in which we're embedded (our conscious, this-is-me story), it seems full of plausibility. On the other hand, when we think of the eschatological story, the covenant/creation story, the new-self story in Christ, we're struck by a sense of implausibility; because these innovative stories fly in the face of the social imaginary and, therefore, of what is plausible. The social imaginary of the West expresses itself as a collective assumption that life is about surviving, about maximizing advantage, about not losing face, about winning, and about being a nice person;[6] life is about relationships, yes, but relationships in which one has the advantage, is able to scan the exits, and can think self-protectively rather than in a self-giving way (which, again, seems implausible in the current social field). Yet, the call of God's kingdom is to do what seems implausible (to love sacrificially as Christ first loved us).

Here's a story (a compilation of many) that catches up some of the key concepts of this chapter. All his life, a man now in his forties has labored for the approval of his father. The latter, an accumulator of material wealth, is a sharp dealer who attends church, weighs in heavily in the financial matters of the church, and marks people by the cars they drive. He knows the Bible, being more impressed by his knowledge of it than by the Bible itself. His

---

5. Barth, *Doctrine of Reconciliation*, 350.
6. Argyris, *Reasoning, Learning, and Action*, 87.

THE STORIED SELF

scriptural knowledge gives him an armamentarium with which to bully his son: "I notice you been getting home by 5:30 most days. You know, the Bible says, 'Let him who does not work not eat' (2 Thess 3:10)." These words hit an anxiety button in the son, who, striving ever more assiduously to meet his father's standard, has developed a constant, one-down view of himself. This "I'm not good enough" story is a dark stream that runs beneath the conscious quotidian. Out of the dark stream rises a miasma of insecurity, an emptiness that is sometimes not assuaged by his wife's efforts to encourage him. A woman at work begins to linger at his office door, prolonging conversations, introducing topics that are foolish to follow. But the interest she shows feels like cool water to the thirst of his insecurity, and he begins to drink.

In a subsequent spiritual conversation with a friend, it emerges that none of this backstory had been available to him. All he was able to tell as his conscious story was "I was feeling kind of low, and this woman seemed into me, and I screwed up." The deeper story only came to light when the friend, having listened for a while, asked, "What do you think was feeding that low feeling you mentioned?" As the backstory about his father's impact became clearer, another backstory emerged: the father, having grown up in abysmal poverty, harbored a story of which he was deeply ashamed: he had stolen his mother's "nerve pills" and sold them on the street to avoid the embarrassment of being assigned to the lunch line with the schoolkids whose meals were government funded.

These stories, again, *were not available*—not to son nor to father—yet they were deeply influential. Influence without knowledge is slavery. These stories cried out to come to the light and be reread by Christ in the flow of the Holy Spirit. Yet, at the same time, they were deeply hidden and craftily used by the flesh. In chapters 4–7, we'll explore the war between the flesh and the Spirit, focusing on a young woman, Sarah. We'll break off and tell others' stories at times, but we'll return to Sarah, using her story to show in an extended way how spiritual conversations work. After each chapter, I'll append some questions to spur the helper's reflection.

CHAPTER 4

Spiritual Conversations and Kingdom

In the Lord's Prayer, we pray, "Thy kingdom come." Sarah had prayed those words hundreds of times, but she was still anxious. When she was six years old, her uncle sneaked into her bedroom, lay down with her, and fondled her. Then he made her fondle him. This sexual abuse went on for years until her uncle moved away. Sarah told no one, yet she felt as though everyone somehow knew her secret. She judged herself as shameful and dirty. Thinking she saw disgust in others' eyes, she wondered, "Did I bring this on myself? Was there something about *me* that brought my uncle to me? How will I ever get clean?" These questions chased one another in her mind, making her anxious.

"Thy kingdom come." How could God's kingdom come into Sarah's anxious heart? In her fear, she held tightly to her secret. Her heart was like a closed fist, and she lived as in a little kingdom with the Secret on the throne. At times, she could feel Jesus knocking on her heart's door. She wanted to fling open the door and rush into Jesus' arms. But another part of her intoned, "Jesus will say, 'You filthy girl! Why were you with your uncle!?'" This voice stole the freedom Jesus wanted for her. It took her captive again to fear and put her back in the kingdom of the Secret.

SPIRITUAL CONVERSATIONS AND KINGDOM

But God is the great King of all! A crucial part of spiritual conversing is listening well so that the helper knows how to light the lamp of God's truth and love in another's dark places. The message is that there is another kingdom where "perfect love casts out fear" (1 John 4:18). In that kingdom, the Secret is dethroned. The helper's role is to invite Sarah on a relational journey from her small kingdom of fear and secrecy to the expansive kingdom of God. "Relational" means that the helper takes the responsibility to develop a heart-to-heart relationship with Sarah.

Sarah struggles with dread. Since "perfect love casts out fear," any of our imperfect loves will strengthen fear. An imperfect love is one that climbs above its station. For example, it's not wrong for Sarah to have a secret; but, as she matures into adulthood, it becomes foolish to elevate protecting that secret over trusting God. Insisting that secrecy is her only hope makes it an idol. Secrecy becomes her "first love" (Rev 3:4 is relevant here). The result of disordered love is that now Sarah has two fears. First, she fears the shame of anyone finding out about her secret. Second, she fears she will be an imperfect servant of her imperfect love, secrecy. The rest of this book shows how the helper brings the message of God's kingdom so that Sarah reaches freedom.

Sarah did try to get help a few years ago. She went to a fellow Christian who didn't listen well, interrupting often to tell Sarah what to do about her anxiety: "Have you tried meditation? Have you tried aromatherapy? Do you have good sleep hygiene? Are you on the right medication?" The helper kept jumping to solutions before understanding anything about the sources of Sarah's anxiety. Instead of thinking, "What is the backstory?" the helper thought, "How do we solve the problems that are presented?" It's sobering to think that we will be helpful at times yet will also miss important opportunities. We will find we always have some growing to do. How do we grow? Consider the following spiritual practices.

UNSTUCK

GOD'S WORD

Though all of us are busy, it is essential to set aside time to spend in God's word. Trying to meditate on God's word in a few spare minutes a day will not sufficiently deepen our character. It is better to start the day with extended personal time in Scripture, because through it God's kingdom comes to have deeper influence on us. When we take time to open our hearts and immerse ourselves in God's word, it actually studies *us*. Heb 4:12 says, "For the word of God is living and active and sharper than any two-edged sword, and piercing as far as the division of soul and spirit, of both joints and marrow, and able to judge the thoughts and the intentions of the heart." To be more effective helpers, we study to be pierced. The piercing, according to this verse, opens us to a judgment as God takes a discerning look at our motivations.

For example, if the helper who didn't listen to Sarah had described the session to a mentor, the conversation might have gone like this:

Mentor: What was driving you quickly to offer so many solutions?

Helper: I really wanted to help.

Mentor: And helping is so important, because . . . ?

Helper: Well, I do want to help, but I think there's something more . . . I think I want to prove I know what I'm doing.

Mentor: Why?

Helper: If I feel incompetent, I get very anxious.

Mentor: Let's say you keep working hard to prove your competence. Who is that really for?

Helper (after a pause): I guess it's really for me.

Mentor: Where is the love in that?

Helper: I guess that's only self-love.

Mentor: How do you feel about that?

Helper (reflecting): I feel pain. I feel, too, that I need to think and pray about this some more.

After further thought and prayer, she remembers that "love is patient" (1 Cor 13:4). She sees that she was impatient as she pressed solutions on Sarah. She feels the Bible judging "the thoughts and intentions of the heart." Feeling pierced yet also more open and hopeful, she knows God wants to help her grow beyond her fear of incompetence. Again, when we seek to help others, we must be honest about what happens inside us. Sarah's helper served the kingdom of competence instead of the kingdom of God.

Of course, sometimes the Bible shows us what is right about us, too. It might reveal our love for God, our love for others, our patience, and so on. Whether God's word exposes wisdom or folly in us, we become drawn to prayer.

PRAYER

Prayer is meant to happen all the time, everywhere. "Pray without ceasing," says 1 Thess 5:17. Prayer equals spiritual breathing. As we take in life's events (like breathing in), we respond with prayer (like breathing out); it helps us move from disarray toward peace. We "let [our] requests be made known to God" (Phil 4:6); or we praise him, we confess sin, we thank him. We also pray for the people we help, asking God for wisdom.

Prayer fosters security. As an illustration of prayer, I think of a barnacle, a little shellfish that attaches itself to hard surfaces underwater. Cement glands in its head attach it firmly to a rock, boat, or pier. Prayer, consistently practiced, cements us more securely to God, reminding us that nothing "shall be able to separate us from the love of God, which is in Christ Jesus our Lord" (Rom 8:39). The influences of other kingdoms reach for us, but love from God calls us back to God's ruling in our lives.

Consistent prayer works at defeating fear. Paul says, "Be anxious for nothing, but in everything by prayer and supplication with thanksgiving let your requests be made known to God. And the peace of God, which surpasses all comprehension, shall guard your hearts and your minds in Christ Jesus" (Phil 4:6–7). Prayer actually defends our hearts and minds when fear invades. Through prayer, we obey wisdom's call: "Watch over your heart with all diligence, / For from it flow the springs of life" (Prov 4:23). In prayer, we keep vigil over our hearts so that pride, lust, selfishness, anxiety, impatience, and unforgiveness find inhospitable soil there. If we fail to guard against these intruders, they infect our "springs of life" and become part of us. As they inhabit us, they tempt us toward self-focus. Prayer involves our battling to cleanse what flows from our hearts so that our words and actions benefit other people.

Let's go back to Sarah. Imagine her helper praying silently during the meeting for two things:

- First, for insight and understanding. Paul sets the example: "I pray that the eyes of your heart may be enlightened so that you may know what is the hope of His calling" (Eph 1:18). "O Lord," she prays as she listens to Sarah, "shine your light into my heart so that I may understand this woman. Give me the 'understanding heart' that Solomon prayed for" (1 Kgs 3:9).

- Second, that the Holy Spirit would impress on her the direction he wants her to go in helping Sarah. She opens to the Spirit's help as she listens both to the Spirit of God and to Sarah. She is less open to amassing evidence that she's competent and more open to wondering about the Spirit's agenda concerning Sarah.

Of course, the helper should at times pray out loud for Sarah, too! Whatever the locus of prayer—aloud or within oneself—the helper's prayers should never come from mere habit simply because of the "religious" setting. Spiritual conversations are not religious. In our prayers, we bring not a religion but a relationship (with Christ) both to the hurting and to the foolish aspects of the soul. Prayer interacts with God's kingdom and brings life to spiritual conversations.

SPIRITUAL CONVERSATIONS AND KINGDOM FELLOWSHIP

The helper who wants to grow in godliness should seek fellowship with other believers. "Fellowship" means to have things in common. The foremost thing believers share is Christ, so fellowship centers on Christ. The question in fellowship is "What is Christ doing in your life and in my life, and how can we help one another along the path of growth he lays out for each of us?" Fellowship is not chatting with other Christians about the weather, the news, or anything that happens to occur to us. Instead, Christians in fellowship take seriously Paul's words: "It was for freedom that Christ set us free; therefore keep standing firm and do not be subject again to a yoke of slavery" (Gal 5:1). Christian fellowship focuses on helping one another increase our freedom in Christ. We are free in two ways:

- First, Christ frees us from having to sin. He frees us from pride and legalism, for example. He frees us from sexual sin. In all these things, we refuse to put on the yoke of bondage again. In other words, we guard against backsliding. Helpers should take care to walk in God-given freedom, for sexual temptations can occur in spiritual conversations as well as temptations to dominate, control, or become passive. Or, as we've seen, to demonstrate competence in service to one's ego.

- Second, Christ frees us for new actions in his name. He frees us to love as he has loved us. He frees us to be patient and to forgive. He frees us to be "kind to one another, tender-hearted, forgiving each other, just as God in Christ also has forgiven you" (Eph 4:32).

Both kinds of freedom—freedom *from* and freedom *for*—deeply challenge us. We cannot practice them well without help from other believers. In true fellowship, we battle for one another through prayer and open discussion. We seek to inculcate the priorities of God's kingdom in one another. Every Christian who aspires to be of help should belong to a community of healing and repentance, a small group in which honesty about personal brokenness can come out in the open without fear of rejection.

UNSTUCK

I have belonged to such a small group for over twenty years. In our case, five men have committed to grow as disciples, and anything is discussable. At the same time, everything is confidential. The norm of confidentiality provides each of us a safe place to reveal uncomfortable material without fear of judgment. In this group I learned the great truth "There's something beyond the pain." Realizing that someone was calling me (and has never stopped, and never will) from beyond the pain was immensely freeing. The realization that "it's only pain" began the trajectory that reached an important height in God's calling from beyond the pain and became an important motif in the third book of this series, *We Hate to Wait*. Without this safe invitation to cough up whatever hair ball is rumbling inside, my journey of dealing with pain would have been deeply impoverished, as would have been my ability to be effective as a helper.

WORSHIP

Worship is another necessary spiritual practice for the helper. Worshiping God means expressing to the Lord how much he impresses us, how God's glory and love inspire awe in us. We worship God by honoring his majesty and compassion, might and mercy, wisdom and grace. When we honor God, we remember that "as for man, his days are like grass; / As a flower of the field; so he flourishes. / When the wind has passed over it, it is no more; / And its place acknowledges it no longer" (Ps 103:15-16). Praising and honoring God humbles us, putting us in our rightful place so that we are not "lording it over those allotted to [our] charge, but proving to be examples to the flock" (1 Pet 5:3). In a way, the helper who pressed solutions on Sarah lorded it over her. The helper's needs dominated the session, and Sarah received little help. When the helper worshiped in the kingdom of competence, the meeting was more about her own benefit than Sarah's. When, in repentance, the helper shifted toward acting as a citizen of heaven, she gave the next session over to the Holy Spirit and to Sarah's well-being.

SPIRITUAL CONVERSATIONS AND KINGDOM

As we sit with someone like Sarah, we see her as a fellow pilgrim. Through the humility of worship, we see that we, too, struggle with life. To Jesus, all of us resemble sheep. Yet, we are called to come alongside others and lead them with compassion. Instead of worshiping power, control, or impressiveness, we worship the Lord.

"But an hour is coming, and now is, when the true worshipers shall worship the Father in spirit and truth; for such people the Father seeks to be His worshipers" (John 4:23). "Spirit" here means the Holy Spirit, and I believe "truth" here means the Truth, Jesus Christ. In other words, Jesus teaches that we worship truly when we worship God as Father, Son, and Holy Spirit. The purpose of worship is to conduct us into the joy of the Trinity. As we rise into this joy, we are made stronger. "Do not be grieved, for the joy of the Lord is your strength," says Neh 8:10. Though Nehemiah knew nothing of the Trinity, he grasped that at the heart of God is a great feast of holy and playful joy. With our greater knowledge—in light of the New Testament—we understand that this feast is Trinitarian. As we saw earlier, the interpenetration of Father, Son, and Holy Spirit generates a flow of God's love that overflows and seeks lodgment in our hearts. In worship, we take part in the celebration. The joy that issues from the feast helps us be strong when life is not going well. Sarah is not looking for a helper who worships having an impressive reputation, or one who is validated by a busy schedule, or one who needs affirming responses from those she helps, or one who can convincingly answer, "Fine!" when someone asks how she is doing. Rather, Sarah is looking for a true worshiper, someone who will not be distracted by such false worship. She is looking for a worshiper who knows something of God's joy and yet understands the weariness of endured pain.

SPIRITUAL WARFARE

The devil strives against every human (to increase inhumanity): "Be of sober spirit, be on the alert. Your adversary, the devil, prowls about like a roaring lion, seeking someone to devour. But resist him, firm in your faith, knowing that the same experiences of suffering are being accomplished by your brethren who are in the world" (1 Pet 5:8–9). The word "adversary" here means someone who opposes you in court. The evil one sneaks in to accuse. Only by being "of sober spirit" can the Christian perceive the accuser's plots. "Gird your minds for action, keep sober in spirit, fix your hope completely on the grace to be brought to you at the revelation of Jesus Christ" (1 Pet 1:13).

Peter, who knew the devil's plots firsthand (Luke 22:31–34), encourages us to "be on the alert" (1 Pet 5:8). Another meaning is "to be awake, to be watchful."[1] Dozing with a hungry lion about would be like a sleepy man crossing a deep ravine on a narrow bridge with no handrails. Peter was this sleepy man as he sat near the fire in the courtyard of the high priest. Looking back decades later, he could see that he'd been deeply unmindful of Satan's skillful use of fear and pressure to tempt him to deny Jesus.

To be of "sober spirit" implies keeping in touch with the Holy Spirit. Paul expresses this alliance with the Holy Spirit by using a comparison with drunkenness: "And do not get drunk with wine, for that is dissipation, but be filled with the Spirit" (Eph. 5:18). For example, Sarah's helper must certainly "not get drunk with wine," but she must also not

- get "drunk" on power,
- get "drunk" on pride,
- get "drunk" on anger,
- get "drunk" on jealousy,
- or get "drunk" on "fixing" Sarah.

Instead, she is to "be filled with the Spirit," coming more and more under the influence of the Holy Spirit, who equips her progressively to "resist [the devil] firm in your faith" (1 Pet 5:9). The word "resist" means to "set oneself against, oppose, resist, withstand."[2] The helper stands against Satan by rejecting his accusations and fleeing to Christ.

1. Abbott-Smith, *Greek Lexicon*, 96.
2. Bauer et al., *Greek-English Lexicon*, 66.

SPIRITUAL CONVERSATIONS AND KINGDOM

In order to become more skilled at resisting the devil, the helper should make a thorough study of Zech 3:1-5. Briefly, the passage presents three characters: the angel of the Lord, Joshua the high priest, and Satan. The devil stands at Joshua's right hand "to accuse him" (Zech 3:1). Making this a courtroom scene, Satan prepares to destroy Joshua with words of death. But listen! The first words in the passage are *not* from Satan. The Lord speaks preemptively: "The Lord rebuke you, Satan! Indeed, the Lord who has chosen Jerusalem rebuke you! Is this not a brand plucked from the fire?" (Zech 3:2). By grace, the Lord snatches Joshua, and every believer, from the fire of judgment. Because of this grace, we possess authority in spiritual battles. The helper will encourage many by telling them, if they believe in Christ, that they are safe from all "the flaming missiles of the evil one" (Eph 6:16). Sarah has been wounded by many fiery darts of Satan as he accuses her of being seductive, dirty, and unlovable. Her helper can clarify for her what it means to seek protection behind her "shield of faith" (Eph 6:16).

Satan never speaks in Zech 3:1-5. In this muting of the devil, the Lord declares that our accuser has no authority to set up court in the believer's life. The devil has to leave, and the scenario becomes a healing one, with the Lord and others gathered around Joshua, who is "clothed with filthy garments and standing before the angel" (Zech 3:3). The filthy clothing indicates that Joshua *is* a sinner, yet as one saved from the judgment fire, he has hope, yet a hope not in himself. What happens next reveals God's forgiveness at full tide. The angel of the Lord speaks: "Remove the filthy garments from him" (Zech 3:4). We hear a voice of authority and command. Then, the angel proclaims, "See, I have taken your iniquity away from you and will clothe you will festal robes" (Zech 3:4). The scene climaxes with Joshua clothed from head to toe in clean robes for feasting and joy (Zech 3:5). Notice: Joshua did *nothing* to earn his new standing. Think of Eph 2:8-9: "For by grace you have been saved through faith; and that not of yourselves, it is the gift of God; not as a result of works, that no one should boast."

Helpers can use Zech 3:1-5 to combat the devil's use of accusation and discouragement in their own lives and the lives of those they help. *Many* labor beneath a crushing load of regret and guilt.

Sins of the past may rise up and mock them. Previous mistakes in trying to help others may do the same. The helper may need to mend her standing with others by making amends to them, but her standing before the Lord stands secure. In Christ, she is declared right before God. In Christ, she wears festal robes because of the joy of having been forgiven fully.

GOD'S WORK IN SPIRITUAL CONVERSATIONS

The fact that God is three in one helps us establish that spiritual conversations offer life in the face of death. As we've seen, the three are Father, Son, and Holy Spirit. The Father makes a life-giving covenant with his people, telling them God is for them, not against them, and making an unconditional commitment to deliver them from sin and death and to give them new life, eternal life. By pressing Sarah with quick solutions, her helper tries to prove her competence. In her heart, Sarah's helper believes that life comes from experiencing herself as competent. Deep down, Sarah will sense this self-serving commitment and, unless the lapse of connection becomes discussable, the relationship will suffer a breach of trust.

In helping others, then, we must remember that the Father seeks to bring real life, not the false life of self-display. God's gift of life involves new hope and joy in living. God's life will someday flower into "Behold, I am making all things new!" (Rev 21:5). In the Old Testament, God says to Israel, "For I know the plans that I have for you . . . plans for welfare and not for calamity, to give you a future and a hope" (Jer 29:11). The Father views the Christian community (the church) as coming together to live this new life, to have "a future and a hope." Meeting together to offer help is where "two or three have gathered together in My name, there I am in their midst" (Matt 18:20). What is the Father doing "in their midst"? Clearing the way for new life to come. God gives new vitality for living from the hope of his shining future.

The focus on new life means that the helper should ask, "Am I a life-giving person? Can God work through me to bring life, or do I block this work somehow?" These questions are not meant to

SPIRITUAL CONVERSATIONS AND KINGDOM

bring pressure but are to invite prayer and self-examination. When Sarah's helper spoke with her mentor, she learned that her concern about proving herself blocked the flow of God's life. Later, in prayer, she put herself in God's hands for cleansing (like Joshua, the high priest), making way for repentance and new life.

In self-examination, we will unearth shortcomings. We need not despair or fall into self-contempt. Both of these simply put the focus back on ourselves. Our security and strength to resist them comes from our standing in Christ, who anchors the Father's covenant. Dying on the cross to bring about the forgiveness of our sins, Christ rose from the grave to defeat death. Since sin and death have no ultimate power over us, we are to "walk in newness of life" (Rom 6:4). As the helper connects and speaks, she should remember the wounds and the resurrection of Jesus Christ. They testify that no power in the world, or outside it, can overcome Jesus. The Bible says of Christ that the Father "put all things in subjection under His feet, and gave Him as head over all things to the church, which is His body, the fulness of Him who fills all in all" (Eph 1:22–23). In this power over all powers, Jesus gives "strength to the weary" (Isa 40:29).

Helping others can bring fatigue. We can assume that Sarah's helper wrestles with principalities and powers. She experiences the pain of the people she helps. She contends with the flesh in their lives and her own. The Holy Spirit brings the fire of passion to thank God for the new, secure identity of believers. The fresh fire of thankfulness kindles our hearts to follow and obey. The Spirit relights our candles in the battle with fatigue. If sometimes tired and discouraged, Sarah's helper can say in her heart, "I am called by a new name" (Isa 43:1). She will do well to wrestle with the questions one author spells out: "By whose authority may I change my name? How do I find the power to silence the old names that seem so apt? What hope is there that I will live up to a new name?"[3] Her answer must be, "I am the beloved child of the Lord himself." The helper will do well to remember this for herself

---

3. Dawson, *New Name*, 12.

and for each person who seeks help. She must understand herself as truly forgiven and set free!

CHAPTER 4 QUESTIONS

1. God's word studies us. Can you think of times when God's word has exposed foolishness in your heart? What was the situation? How can this exposure help you in your helping of others?

2. "In true fellowship, we battle for one another through prayer and open discussion." What can you do as a helper to develop at least one relationship marked by open discussion, honesty, and transparency?

3. Based on Zech 3:1–5, how do you intend to help yourself reject the accusations of Satan?

CHAPTER 5

How Does the Helper Help?

Let's imagine Sarah's helper reflecting on this question. First, she must remember that Sarah bears the image of God. Second, she must remember that Sarah is also a fallen sinner.

THE IMAGE OF GOD

Now, Sarah has come for her second meeting. Though she felt pushed and interrupted by the helper, which led her to reveal nothing about her past, she thought the helper wasn't intentionally harmful. Sarah did have some anxiety about being bombed with solutions again. Of course, Sarah does not know that the helper sought a mentor and that God has been working.

Since God is now freeing the helper from her striving for competence, she has found herself reflecting more on the truth of how God sees Sarah. She recalls that Sarah bears the image of God. And being created in God's image confers crucial benefits.

UNSTUCK

Dignity

In the ancient world, only the great kings were likened to the so-called gods. But the true God makes all men and women to reflect who he is, to show his image:

> Then God said, "Let Us make man in Our image, according to Our likeness; and let them rule over the fish of the sea and over the birds of the sky and over the cattle and over all the earth, and over every creeping thing that creeps on the earth." And God created man in His own image; in the image of God He created him. Male and female He created them. (Gen 1:26-27)

Because this is true, all men, women, and children have dignity and value. Sarah, in spite of the abuse that devastated her, is endowed with God-given, unconditional dignity and value. These are indestructible.

We learn in Gen 1 that God made men and women in God's image, but it does not say anything about abilities like intelligence, memory, or will. If these qualities made up God's image, then Satan himself would reflect God's image! Gen 1:27 simply says, "And God created man in His own image, in the image of God He created him, male and female He created them." This passage, along with the Hebrew words selected for "male" and "female," provide rich reflection on the image of God.

The Hebrew for "male" comes from a word that means "remember." It can also mean "monument" (for example, erecting a monument in memory of a person or event). Moreover, it can mean to mention or point out and to be sharp (as in making a sharp distinction). It can also refer to the male sex organ.[1]

The Hebrew for "female" comes from a word that means "to bore into" and is kin to a word that means to make holes, to pierce. Its wider meaning reflects ideas of being pierced, having depth, receiving, and being filled.[2]

---

1. Brown et al., *Hebrew and English Lexicon*, 269-71.
2. Brown et al., *Hebrew and English Lexicon*, 666.

HOW DOES THE HELPER HELP?

The image of God lies not in the male or the female but in the *differences* in the fields of meaning regarding these Hebrew words for "male" and "female." God is spirit, so God is neither male nor female. But, in creating the world, God chooses to reflect *through* maleness one attribute of God's nature and *through* femaleness another attribute. Maleness reflects his strength, or majesty; femaleness reflects his glory, or beauty. When male and female come together in marriage, they are a picture sermon about God. Moreover, each learns from the other so that men grow in compassion and women grow in directness.[3]

These reflections point to important conclusions about God's making us in his image:

1. God designed humans to be both strong and nurturing. Sarah's uncle was too weak to be strong and mature for her but instead was brutal and certainly not nurturing.

2. God intends for male and female to be gifts to one another. Sarah's uncle could have chosen to bring gifts of caring and safety to her.

3. Men are to call women away from despair (because beauty often suffers in this world), while women are to call men toward responsibility (because men are tempted to worship power). Sarah is beauty suffering.

4. God means for humans to live in hope (beauty will survive and thrive, and power can become humble, self-giving protectiveness). Sarah's counselor needs to reflect on how to give her hope.

5. God designs humans to live in covenant with him and relationship with one another.[4] Sarah's uncle brutally shattered any sense of interpersonal covenant.

These ideas should influence how Sarah's counselor works to help her.

---

3. Shores, "Image of God," 126–31.
4. Crabb, *Inside-Out*, 66.

UNSTUCK

The first truth—that God designed humans to be both strong and nurturing—leads the helper to ask questions like these:

- Is the man taking responsibility to protect his family as Jesus would? For example, where was Sarah's father when her uncle was abusing her?
- Does the man avoid discussing important matters because they make him uncomfortable?
- Is the man cold and distant? Is the woman cold and distant? Are either of them overbearing?
- Is the man so friendly that he never faces conflict?
- Does the woman show and teach kindness (Prov 31:26)?

The second truth—that God intends for male and female to be gifts to one another—could lead the helper to ask questions such as:

- Is the one I'm helping a quarrelsome person? If so, why? What's the backstory?
- If married, is the couple competing with one another for outcomes that reveal idolatrous values (for example, competing to be right and prove the other wrong)? If so, why?

The third truth—men are to call women away from despair; women are to call men to responsibility—could lead the helper to wonder:

- Has the woman's beauty of soul (as well as her body) been attacked, abused, or manipulated? Sarah's situation shows the plight of beauty in a fallen world.
- Has the man been allowed to act irresponsibly? Childishly? Intimidatingly?
- Is the man developing a vision of what it means when Paul says, "Husbands, love your wives as Christ loved the church and gave Himself up for her" (Eph 5:25)? Is he becoming a man with whom beauty (of all sorts) is safe? Treating a woman as an object tramples God's glory underfoot.

HOW DOES THE HELPER HELP?

The fourth truth—God means for humans to live in hope—could lead to these questions:

- Is the person I'm helping open to learning greater trust in the Lord? If not, what blocks the way?
- Is this person learning to put every situation under God's standard of truth?
- Is he or she learning that the believer is never finally trapped, that God has always provided "the way of escape" (2 Cor 10:13)?
- Is he or she learning freedom from the bondage of sin?

The fifth truth—God designs humans to live in covenant with him and relationship with one another—could lead the helper to ask:

- Is the person I'm helping willing to connect with others and to not be isolated?
- Does he or she realize the importance of being for his fellow humans and praying about what it means to do them good as God would see the good?
- Is he or she learning to forgive?
- Is he or she learning unconditional love?

Clearly, the Trinitarian, relational God of Scripture urges us to grow into loving disciples who care about relationships.

The helper keeps in mind that Jesus seeks to form these five qualities in his people. He or she thinks of them as the fruit of new life that God longs to form in each believer through the work of the Holy Spirit (again, see Jas 4:5 for more on this longing in God).

Thirsting and Searching

Although created in God's image, we live in a world broken by sin. Our likeness to God means we long for love and significance, yet we live in a world often marked by attack and withdrawal. We sense that we are "strangers and exiles" on the earth (Heb 11:13). Living in a fallen world hits us like a shock wave (or, it *should*) and makes us cry out, "O God, Thou art my God; I shall seek Thee earnestly; / My soul thirsts for Thee, my flesh yearns for Thee / In a dry and weary land where there is no water" (Ps 63:1). This psalm tells us that the shock we experience takes the form of an urgent thirst.

A helper must continually think, "I speak with a thirsty soul in a sinful, and thus competitive, world." Because humans have a soul thirst, we search urgently for something to quench it. The helper must ask, "How does this person use wrong means to satisfy thirst?" To help people truly, we must think in these biblical categories: God's image, thirst, search, foolishness.

Satan tempted Adam and Eve to doubt God's goodness, persuading them to believe that something other than God could provide for them better than God could. Suggesting that God had withheld important information, he declared, "For God knows that in the day you eat from it [the tree of the knowledge of good and evil] your eyes will be opened, and you will be like God, knowing good and evil" (Gen 3:5). Thus, he tempted Adam and Eve to believe that God cannot be trusted. He sold them the idea that unassisted human reason and will could replace God. Then, people could take charge of their own lives and decide how to quench their deep thirst. Of course, this is the heart of fallenness. When Adam and Eve ate from the tree, they drank from an enticing but poisoned well. Later, Israel—God's own people—often abandoned God to search for their own wells. Appalled and agonized, God cries out in Jer 2:13, "For My people have committed two evils: / They have forsaken Me, / The fountain of living waters, / To hew for themselves cisterns, / Broken cisterns, / That can hold no water."

Each Person Is a Story

Six-year-old Sarah lies sleeping. When her uncle wakes her by touching between her legs, her internal world explodes. Pain and shame pour in like lava into a delicate teacup. Her small body and tender soul can't *begin* to handle the evil. Life turns inward. For years, she walks with eyes downcast, shoulders slumped. She

HOW DOES THE HELPER HELP?

becomes fearful. Her thirst for God gets confused with her search for safety. Of course, safety is good, but striving for it as the highest goal of a lifetime traps Sarah in a small story. A desire for order can become a demand that disorders. "Walls have become ever closer, and hearts ever narrower."[5] The more her protecting walls draw inward, the narrower her life becomes. The big events are too big for Sarah. She retreats to safety at all costs. Big events can trap us in small stories. But big events (like abuse) *don't* make our stories too big for God.

Every one of us experiences thirst. Every one of us searches to quench that thirst. But every search differs. One person may try to slake it by gaining power. Another may seek riches. Another may seek fame. Another may want to be pitied. Another may seek attention. Why do people search to quench their thirst in so many ways? Because every person lives in two important stories, a big one and a little one. Here, we come at our earlier ideas of story from a different angle.

The big story, which includes everyone, is that God created the world. The Creator God made everything good, including people. When sin invaded the world through Adam and Eve, the world fell, twisting away from God. Through sin's invasive seductiveness, we became blind to our true need. But God still loves the world, and he sets his "face like flint" to rescue his beloved creation (with Isa 50:7 in mind). God sent his son, Jesus Christ, to help us, to be the water of life, to deliver us from evil. In the sweep of this story, we find hope but are not free as yet from the realities of sin and darkness. Every person harbors a nagging homesickness for God, yet is at the same time blinded to his or her need for God.

The little story is the story of each person's life. These stories hold many things: hopes, dreams, relationships, disappointments, joy, struggle, laughter, and sorrow. In the little story, we learn that life carries pain. We also learn, like Adam and Eve, to escape the pain by taking control. People work hard to overcome problems in their own clever resourcefulness. As we saw earlier, "There is a way which seems right to a man, but its end is the way of death" (Prov

---

5. Käsemann, *Jesus Means Freedom*, 99.

14:12). If an action leads to the way of death, how can it seem so right? In answer, the Bible says we think foolishly. We literally don't see the forms of death that come with selfish choices. How have we become foolish? This question brings us to the second truth a helper must remember, that the same person who bears God's image also lives as a fallen sinner.

THE MEANING OF "FALLEN SINNER"

Sarah focuses now entirely on safety. Without realizing it, she makes a vow: "I will never trust another person." The big events in her life lead her to make a big promise to herself. Ironically, fulfilling the big promise will make her life small. We all desire safety. Sarah's *desire* for safety is good, but as a *demand* that governs her life, it becomes a master she must serve. Though she loves the Lord, she has a competing lord in her life. That false lord lures her into misplaced dependency. But, as Jesus says, "No one can serve two masters" (Matt 6:24). The other master in her life lures Sarah into her own rules for living and leads her astray.

"All of us like sheep have gone astray, / Each of us has turned to his own way" (Isa 53:6). Turning to our own way means we replace God with our personal willpower. Our hearts twist away from him; we pursue our own paths. "The heart is more deceitful than all else and is desperately sick; who can understand it?" (Jer 17:9). As we have seen in the first three volumes, the Bible often calls this twist in the heart "the flesh." The flesh is our selfish self that goes against God. It works to avoid pain and replace God. Ripening like a dark fruit inside, the flesh combines many ways of finding safety and control. So numerous are the possible combinations that we each develop a unique flesh pattern, like a fingerprint. When Sarah meets with her, the helper should seek to discern this fingerprint.

The flesh thinks about itself and does not love well. Love may bring pain, so in our flesh, we often avoid loving. Instead, we think first about protecting ourselves. Since the flesh is self-concerned, it tends to bypass what is good for others. In this way, the flesh brings pain to relationships, turning them often into places of suffering.

HOW DOES THE HELPER HELP?

But God loves relationships. To repeat: within God's own oneness, God lives in relationship, each member of the Trinity (Father, Son, and Holy Spirit) loving the others and experiencing love in return. God created us to share that self-giving love with God and with one another. But sin deceives us into believing we should protect ourselves from others and from God. We care about our own outcomes more than about God and others.

The helper should be careful to think about God's love for relationships. Working with someone like Sarah, she should ask herself:

1. Have I taken the log out of my own eye?
2. Have I learned how I walk in the flesh in self-deceiving ways?
3. Have I prayed about this secrecy of sin and asked the Lord to lead me to repentance?
4. Have I examined my own relationships?
5. Have I explored before the Lord my own failures of love?

Only as we grow in Christ can we discern how the Lord wants relationships to work. Sarah's helper also needs to listen to learn how Sarah has been wounded in relationships. Helping must focus on learning about the past and present relationships in Sarah's life. Learning about these relationships unveils to the helper Sarah's experiences of love and lack of love. Sarah's story must teach the helper a wide and wise view of her life. The helper learns about pain and courage but also about how the flesh uses pain for its own purposes.

When we walk in the flesh, we live against ourselves, against others, and against God. We bury our longing to love the Lord. We hurt relationships. We quench the Holy Spirit. Since we live against ourselves, we live with a war inside: "For the flesh sets its desire against the Spirit, and the Spirit against the flesh; for these are in opposition to one another" (Gal 5:17). This war inside brings misery, and the misery often comes out as symptoms that others can see and that we sometimes see in ourselves. A symptom indicates disease. A disease can be of the body but also of the soul and of relationships.

Therefore, people-helping that influences mere behavioral change is not sufficient. Remember David's saying, "Behold, Thou dost desire truth in the innermost being. / And in the hidden part Thou wilt make me know wisdom" (Ps 51:6). In helping, we seek wisdom about how to speak into the war in the heart.

Recently, I reflected back on Ted, a man who had just left my counseling office. I thought, "He spoke many words with force, like a great waterfall. And, as I look back on our time, I now see that Ted often referred to his accomplishments as if giving his résumé." I wondered about why he would need these actions. I asked myself how they protect him. I wondered how his flesh may drive these behaviors. I prayed for wisdom. I also reflected on the pain in Ted that might fuel these behaviors. Does he use his words as armor, because he hides serious wounds? Is his armor really a form of bandaging himself? How might the Lord want to whisper that he himself wants to pour "oil and wine" on this man's wounds (see Luke 10:34)? I prayed for understanding.

If Ted hides behind armor and bandages his own wounds, he acts foolishly. God himself seeks to be his healer and shepherd. As Ted's helper, I pray to help this man understand what blocks him from trusting God more deeply with his pain and his sin.

The War

Ted is in a war, because, to repeat, "the flesh sets its desire against the Spirit, and the Spirit against the flesh; for these are in opposition to one another" (Gal 5:17). Ted wants me to see his power (through his many words) and his goodness (through his résumé). The flesh urges him to make an impressive show, but the Spirit wants him to be open and honest. This is the war.

The gospel of Luke tells the story of Jesus coming to visit two sisters. The Lord arrives at mealtime, so the older sister, Martha, runs back and forth getting the meal ready. She becomes impatient with the many tasks and finally bursts out with forceful words: "Lord, do You not care that my sister has left me to do all the serving alone?" (Luke 10:40). She demands that the Lord tell Mary, her

HOW DOES THE HELPER HELP?

sister, to help her. But Jesus refuses, saying, "Mary has chosen the good part, which shall not be taken away from her" (Luke 10:42), for she sits at Jesus' feet, learning from him.

The flesh urges Ted to be like Martha, of whom Jesus said, "Martha, Martha, you are worried and bothered about so many things" (Luke 10:41). The Holy Spirit whispers and urges Ted to be like Mary and to obey Jesus when he says elsewhere, "But seek first His kingdom and His righteousness; and all these things shall be added to you" (Matt 6:33). Jesus says this because his kingdom feeds our hungry hearts. The shock of living in a sinful world makes us cry inside. Our hearts starve in a fallen world. Their hunger comes out in tears. Jesus is the bread of life (John 6:35). Our souls weep for this bread.

When Mary sat at Jesus' feet feeding on his words, her soul found its resting place. He satisfied her aching hunger. Later, she responded beautifully: she "took a pound of very costly, genuine spikenard ointment, and anointed the feet of Jesus, and wiped his feet with her hair, and the house was filled with the fragrance of the ointment" (John 12:3). She answered with gratitude and humility to Jesus' words of life. She loved Jesus and forgot about herself, and in forgetting about herself, she served him gladly. She no longer lived in conflict with herself or the world around her. Anchored in Jesus, she learned self-giving.

In spiritual conversations, we invite people to stop giving too much weight to lesser things. Think of Ted. We long for him to feel less at war inside and more at peace—to feel the "peace of God, which surpasses all comprehension." Then this peace may "guard your hearts and your minds in Christ Jesus" (Phil 4:7). In the gospel of Luke, Mary's heart found the shelter of God's peace in Jesus. My prayer for Ted is the same: "Lord, may he leave his pain in your hands and leave behind his foolish armor and self-bandaging. May you end his war and grant him peace." This vision for him becomes part of our conversation.

UNSTUCK

Staying Stuck

Mary poured the ointment onto Jesus' feet on an evening when his hosts had "made Him a supper there; and Martha was serving; but Lazarus was one of those reclining at the table with Jesus" (John 12:2). Notice that Martha stays busy even though Jesus earlier had encouraged her not to be "worried and bothered about so many things" (Luke 10:41). Why does Martha still move about like a busy bee? Why hasn't she valued Jesus' encouraging her to rest and be still? In other words, why do we often resist change? Why do we stay stuck in familiar patterns of walking in the flesh?

Returning to Sarah's story, we see how fear can capture a person. She busies herself worrying. She sees rest and stillness as uncomfortable. The Bible says, "We love, because He first loved us" (1 John 4:19). Therefore, if we forget that God walks with us, we neglect to love others. Without a constant reminder of God's love, we love poorly. When we forget God's rich, prior, and unconditional love for us, concern for ourselves rules our lives. The helper, then, must emphasize the love of God in Jesus Christ, the love poured out by the Holy Spirit. She must turn often to say, "And hope does not disappoint, because the love of God has been poured out within our hearts through the Holy Spirit who was given to us" (Rom 5:5). What casts out fear? Deeply drinking of God's love, of that unceasing fountain.

As we grow in Christ, we relish his magnificent love for us. We understand that "there is no fear in love; but perfect love casts out fear, because fear involves punishment, and the one who fears is not perfected in love" (1 John 4:18). God is the one who could punish, but since Christ has turned aside God's wrath by taking it upon himself (what great love!), the believer has no reason to fear. That is why fear doesn't belong to love. Love removes fear of God's rejection. If God will not judge and punish us, we need fear nothing else. The greatest disaster has been turned aside. Salvation shelters us from all penalty. Jesus said, "And do not fear those who kill the body, but are unable to kill the soul; but rather fear Him who is able to destroy both soul and body in hell" (Matt 10:28). Who is the one able to destroy body and soul? God. Yet, God also has sent Jesus to absorb that destruction! The believer now has the foundation to be more and more free from fear.

God's love gives life and hope to the heart. God's love anchors Christian helping. The helper must not only speak about God's love but also show that love to the people who come for help. He or she would do well to pray for the qualities of love described in 1 Cor 13:4–8. Sad to say, Martha had become the heroine of tasks instead of the lover of people.

Wisdom

To engage in spiritual conversations, we need divine wisdom to provide real help to others. Wisdom begins in the fear of the Lord. "The fear of the Lord is the beginning of wisdom, / And the knowledge of the Holy One is understanding" (Prov 9:10). As we worship and honor the Lord, reverence makes a space in our hearts for his wisdom to live and grow. Reverence quiets our ego-driven urgency to engineer the outcomes we demand. We walk with a Lord who travels with us, speaking his word in our hearts about how to counsel people like Sarah or Ted. Wisdom is skill in living the truth we know. Wisdom also knows the flesh's mission to make us raise lesser loves above God. The flesh corrupts us to take control, like Martha, but the Spirit desires that we rest in Jesus, like Mary. Wisdom knows there is a war. God's love helps wisdom fight the battle of Spirit with flesh. The helper longs to enter the battle alongside people like Sarah. He or she joins the battle by

1. understanding Sarah's flesh pattern;
2. prayerfully discerning how to expose the flesh pattern to light;
3. calling her to repentance of the flesh pattern;
4. encouraging the true, Spirit-led aspect of the believer to "walk in newness of life" (Rom 6:4) and to "forsake childish things" (1 Cor 13:11);
5. teaching her that the pain reflects a thirst that reveals who she really is: one who bears God's image;

6. setting the example by wanting God above all lesser gods (Exod 20:3) and helping Sarah in doing the same;

7. pointing always to the love of God in Christ Jesus poured out by the Holy Spirit;

8. and coming alongside her with compassion for her pain.

Wisdom includes paying attention to what happens in the helper's own heart. Here is an example. Recently, I was trying to help a man see that the world is a place of sorrow. This thought disturbed him, and he strongly resisted it. After more conversation, he told me I was not helping him at all. I responded sharply, saying, "You always block me!"

The edge in my words hurt him. If I had paid attention to my heart, I would have noticed that his expression of frustration made me feel weak and useless. I spoke sharply in order to feel strong again. I should have been stopping to reflect on why he felt that my words about the world's sorrow didn't help. Instead of listening more carefully, I was walking in fear—the fear of being powerless. To help myself feel powerful, I spoke careless words that caused needless pain. And I thought about myself more than about him at that moment.

Wisdom required that I speak with him later about what I had discovered about myself. Discussing this with him accomplished two things. First, it showed him that I am not an "expert," not his superior. Instead, we walk as fellow pilgrims in need of Jesus Christ. Second, it showed us a place to begin again. The next time we talked, we began with the moment he said that I wasn't helping. We went more slowly. I call this "a reflective loop." We sometimes make mistakes in helping, and we should not cover them up but instead learn from them. We return (or loop back) to the point the mistake was made. The reflective loop is part of wisdom.

HOW DOES THE HELPER HELP?
CHAPTER 5 QUESTIONS

1. "God intends for male and female to be gifts to one another." How might this idea change our view of the opposite gender? How would you seek to live out this truth about male and female not being adversaries?

2. How does believing we must protect ourselves from others lead us to walk in the flesh? What is one way you could set the example by protecting yourself less often?

3. Read Luke 10:38–42. How would you use this passage to lead someone who seeks help to grow toward seeking and loving God above all?

CHAPTER 6

The Facets of Trouble

When people seek help, they will not say, "I believe I have a flesh pattern that is hiding in me." They will not say, "I believe I have a deep wound in my soul that makes me doubt that God loves me." Instead, they say things like, "My son is beginning to be rebellious and only wants to hang out with his friends. They may all be using alcohol. When we discipline him, he rebels even more. What do we do?"

At this point, we must understand the idea of urgency. When a parent says, "My son is out of control and tearing our family apart," the helper may feel that it is urgent to do something right away. Of course, this is what parents want. Through their words, they urge the helper to solve the problem.

The helper must pay attention inside his heart. Does he feel:

- a desire to make a difference?
- a desire to gain a reputation for effectiveness?
- a concern not to seem incompetent?
- worried he will look uncaring?

These are signs that he should slow down. He should think in the categories we have been learning in this book. For example, he could remember

THE FACETS OF TROUBLE

- that every person, while made in God's image, lives in a fallen world as a thirsty soul. He could then remember
- that everyone is searching. He can begin to wonder
- what the parents have been searching to find through their children. He can wonder
- what the son is searching to find in his friends. He can then wonder
- what the wounds are in each person's heart. And he can wonder
- how the flesh has used these wounds to drive each family member on a wrong search.

Of course, the parents want the problem solved quickly. They are in pain. But the helper helps by teaching them that God doesn't want pain to drive us but to teach us. God wants pain to lose its sovereignty, becoming—instead of a lord—a teacher that alerts us to the deeper suffering entailed by our being ensconced in fallenness. God desires that we understand our deep foolishness in coping with that pain. Then we can repentantly develop habits that lead to the freedom to love well. With these things in mind, we will explore six common problems to see what we can learn.

Note: the descriptions below are not "diagnostic." That is, they do not fit the diagnostic categories in the *Diagnostic and Statistical Manual of Mental Disorders* (now in its fifth edition).[1] Spiritual conversations can, I believe, address any struggle in life in a way that makes a substantial difference. However, if the internal conflicts (the embedded story) remain stubbornly in place as the helping relationship unfolds, the helper may need prayer and discernment (including consulting with others) about referring the other to professional counseling.

---

1. American Psychiatric Association, *Manual of Mental Disorders*.

UNSTUCK

MARRIAGE

Sarah meets a man, love develops between them, and they marry. But soon, her husband wants to control her. He tells her how to cook, how to clean, what to wear, what friends she can have. He keeps her from her parents, brothers, and sisters. After a year of this, Sarah feels like a dog on a leash. She becomes deeply depressed.

Whole cultures have fallen asleep about God's will for marriage. They see marriage as a relationship to meet needs and control risk. Beginning with Adam and Eve, we are banished from our true home. We become needy people. The risks in marriage come from the fact that sin portrays others as storehouses full of goods yet also as threats. We feel both entitled to each other and afraid of each other. We feel entitled to search the other for what we need. At the same time, we feel afraid of rejection, being used, being abandoned. The Bible contradicts these entitlements, viewing the spousal relationship neither as a heap of goods nor as an army of threats.

Sarah's husband controls risk by controlling Sarah. If he can make her into an obedient doll, he will never have to worry about the challenges of a true relationship. He will never have to stretch his mind to understand her opinions, her dreams, her suffering. Having the goal of being comfortable on his own terms, he will never have to awaken to these realities.

People in marriage need an awakening. Marriage must come under the Lord's command: "Awake, sleeper, / And arise from the dead, / And Christ will shine on you" (Eph 5:14). The helper deals with this need by prompting the couple to rise from the sleep of selfishness. He or she helps them see that Christ's way means working together instead of competing with one another. Spouses cannot work together if each pursues lesser gods. The lesser gods make the other spouse look threatening. Only as they fix their eyes on Jesus; only as they put off the old man and put on the new man can they be united (Eph 4:22-24; Heb 12:2). This is how the "two shall become one" (Gen 2:24).

A second need in marriage is to realize that the flesh is like an arrow that shoots toward its own goals. We discussed in depth the drive of the flesh in the second book of this series, *Cleanup*. Pain

THE FACETS OF TROUBLE

launches that arrow toward its goals with great force. As the flesh moves through life, it ignores the wants and needs of others. God intends for marriage to expose the selfishness of this arrow.

When two people marry, they mingle their flesh arrows. This mingling happens in three ways. Picture one arrow inside another one. This is the first pattern. The stronger flesh arrow has dominated and absorbed the weaker one. The weaker has accepted the domination. The weak arrow opts to concede, but both are wrong. Sarah's husband is wrong to dominate her, but she is also wrong in her passive acceptance of his control. Her assumptions about submission are not biblical.

In the second pattern, picture two arrows coming against each other. In this picture, the flesh arrows seek contradictory goals. There is constant conflict as the arrows collide. Both are wrong. Suppose Sarah decided to quarrel with her husband every time she felt controlled. The marriage would deteriorate into a constant war with no hope.

In the third pattern, the two flesh arrows move along beside each other. The couple exists together, but the two are not close. Busy with separate visions of life, their flesh patterns create distance. Their hearts hide from each other as they live parallel lives. Both are wrong.

The helper watches for these flesh-arrow patterns and helps the couple see how they hurt the marriage. He or she then invites them to imagine what life could be without the patterns, asking them, too, what repentance might look like.

Sarah sought help, being full of weariness. Her life lacked meaning. She had the sadness called depression. The helper wanted to see her husband, too, but he refused to attend.

Through a series of spiritual conversations, Sarah realized that she kept quiet to avoid conflict. She saw that she protected herself instead of doing the best for the marriage. Her years of being too silent meant she fell short as the helpmate Scripture describes (Gen 2:18), because she had not ventured to help her husband with his *character*. The Holy Spirit brought conviction about her passive silence. She woke up to her responsibility. She began quietly but firmly to "[speak] the truth in love" (Eph 4:15) with the goal of helping her husband see that his control had hurt him by hurting the marriage. He had robbed himself of a true helpmate. Moreover, he could not grow "to a mature man, to the measure of the stature which belongs to the fulness of Christ" (Eph 4:13). Was Sarah running a risk in speaking truth lovingly to her husband? Yes. On the other hand, she was taking a risk by being passive as well: the risk of losing entirely her voice, her freedom to speak.

If the spouse is physically abusive, that's an entirely different story. The helper should then shift toward helping the woman find local women's resource agencies that specialize in opening a path to freedom for battered women.

DEPRESSION

When someone has lost something important that he feels he cannot do without, depression may be the outcome. We just considered Sarah. Her husband's anger had trained her to be silent. She became sad to the point of depression. She was exhausted, having lost any hope that she could influence her marriage or her life. She felt like a machine, only good for doing tasks. She had given up all hope of true closeness with her husband, and she did not know how to get that hope back.

Another way to describe depression is that it's a deep sadness that brings a person to a standstill. The depressed person simply doesn't want to move, finding everyday living to be a massive climb on an endless mountain.

The unique features of depression, then, are as follows:

1. A depressed person has lost something precious, and he or she does not know how to get it back.

2. A depressed person finds movement intolerable.

Both ideas give the helper important ways to understand the needs of the depressed one. The first idea shows that help must center on providing hope. But the hope must be fed to the person as if with a spoon. This is because the pain in the depressed person fills the mind. The helper cannot accomplish much by teaching

THE FACETS OF TROUBLE

the depressed one, because the pain is so great that the mind cannot hold much more.

How can we, in spiritual conversation, approach this type of pain? Two things: first, listen carefully and patiently. Even if the other is silent, one can listen to the silence, because silence says many things. It can "speak" of despair, regret, self-hatred, struggles to trust, hatred of others, anger at God, confusion, fear. After a long silence, the counselor can say, "I am here." And then, "What do you think your silence might be telling you?" Then, listen patiently if the other speaks. The more the depressed one feels heard, the more he or she thinks, "Maybe I really do matter to someone."

Hope began for Sarah when she discovered that she mattered to another person and then to God. Though she had lost something important and didn't know how to get it back, the hope that someone cared, and that God cared, started a new story. She learned that God is always up to something good. What is God up to? God desires to turn our hearts into a work space where, gradually, we grow to resemble his son, Jesus. Since nothing can stop God from working "all things . . . together for good" (Rom 8:28), the new story can begin at any moment. In her new story, Sarah realized that God uses pain (against Satan's will) to form her into someone more like Jesus. She discerned that, on a deep subfloor of her heart, there was something indestructible: a longing to know the God who had so intimately perceived her need by sending Christ. Isaiah 64:1 cries out, "O that Thou wouldst rend the heavens and come down." God answers that plea by sending Christ as the invasion that invades the invader, sin. That means there is always something beyond the pain. God's work embraced Sarah from beyond the pain. That hope invited her to risk leaning into God's story of newness.

The second idea (that depression stops movement) gives the helper two more ways to help. The first is to help the depressed person think of stopped movement as resting. He may say, "Though you do not want to do anything, this is not all bad. Something deep inside needs a rest. What in your life has made you desperately need a rest?" Sarah's answer was that she needed rest from her diseased and painful thinking. This gave the helper many opportunities to model and discuss the fresh thinking of

UNSTUCK

Scripture. The helper here used the principle "Be transformed by the renewing of your mind" (Rom 12:2).

The second thing a helper can do, after a time, is give the depressed one small assignments that require movement. "Go to your neighbor's and borrow an egg." Or "Walk one hundred steps away from your home and come back." Or simply, "Make up your bed." Or "Go to the grocery store and come back. Don't do any shopping, that's for another day." Or "Bake some bread today or tomorrow." Or "If that is too much, simply look up a bread-making recipe."

These assignments remind the person what movement feels like. The depressed one will have little desire to do them, yet doing them little by little increases the desire to move. Movement makes one feel effective. If we could compare depression to a large, dark bush filling the mind, active movement prunes the bush. Feeling effective makes one feel that life is not over.

ANXIETY

Anxiety is fear that has no clear cause. If, say, a dog rushes at you, attempting to bite, fear has a clear cause. But if you imagine attacking dogs everywhere and tremble even to get out of bed, that is anxiety. The unique feature of anxiety is a sense of threat. But the threat is unclear (there is no actual dog at the moment). Under this indefinable threat, the person senses a risk that has no remedy. That is, the risk is there, but the person thinks his abilities cannot meet it. Fear also involves risk, but the risk is easy to see. If I must cross a rope bridge with no rails over a lake of crocodiles, that is a clear risk. Anyone would feel fear in that place. But the risks that cause anxiety are difficult to see at first.

Here, we leave Sarah for a moment to tell my own story of anxiety, a story that sheds light on this idea of unclear risk. I had been working at a seminary for a year, enjoying teaching classes and directing the counseling services for students and faculty. Everything seemed fine. One night, I had an attack of anxiety as sudden as a thunderstorm. I didn't know what to do, but each night I prayed and wrote in my journal and read my Bible (especially the

THE FACETS OF TROUBLE

Psalms). After about six anxious weeks of haggardly walking the floor at night, crying out to God and reflecting, I came to see that I was desperately afraid that I didn't belong at such a well-known school. I was terrified the other faculty would discover that I was a fake, that I did not know what I was doing. Could I keep hiding the fact that I was an impostor? This was my threat.

Here, we return to two ideas we've discussed. First, every human bears God's image. Second, we are all fallen sinners who often think and act foolishly. As one made in God's image, I longed to make a difference in students' lives, working effectively like the other faculty. But as a sinner, I foolishly thought that the only way to measure up was to drive myself hard, working late into the night and hiding my uncertainties. I thought that I had to conceal my ignorance and not reach out for help. I felt the risk of falling short and foolishly tried to meet that risk by working in my own strength. I should have gone to the Lord with my uncertainty and should have reached out for help. It would have been wise for me to find an older faculty mentor or to seek a Christian counselor in the city.

My foolish flesh pattern consisted of hiding my fears, working beyond my own strength, and failing to seek wise helpers. As I grew and repented of these patterns, the Lord provided a small group of men who are wise friends. These friends, as I've mentioned before, meet once a week and share anything with one another. We take each one's fears, sins, confusions, and hurts to the Lord. This group of five men has been a great blessing to me.

Helpers must listen carefully to the anxious person and pray that the threat deep in the heart will be revealed. They must also pray to understand the foolish ways in which that person has tried to manage the threat. Anxiety may occur suddenly (as in my case), because the person's wrong ways of dealing with the threat have stopped working or have made the person too tired to make any more efforts.

UNSTUCK

ANGER

Anger and plunder go together. In an imaginary land grew two trees filled with golden and silvery light, like sun and moon. Their immense beauty died when a gigantic, grotesque spider attacked the trees and sucked out all their light. The people in great wrath chased the spider through their now-dim land.[2] The story shows the link between plunder and anger. Anger means something has been taken.

But anger must not turn into rage. Anger can easily rot into rage, because it rots into self-concern and bitterness. Rage is not simply a more intense anger. Instead, rage has different goals than anger. How do the two differ? Certainly, anger is the more constructive, as shown by the following:

- Anger wants to push constructively against evil.
- Anger mourns over sin (that of oneself and of others).
- Anger requires the capacities of a mature adult.
- Anger remembers that people are people, never objects.

On the other hand, the destructive nature of rage is evident:

- Rage works to shield the fragile self and isn't picky about its methods.
- Rage simply wants to push the other person far away.
- Rage is the emotion of a threatened child.
- Rage loses sight of others as persons and treats them as objects.

Anger and rage have something in common in that they arise because of a blocked goal. For example, a driver may feel anger because another driver's recklessness almost causes a crash. His anger reveals that his goal of a more ordered and loving world is far from being fulfilled. Another driver may feel rage because his goal is to have everyone stay out of his way as though he owns the road. In both cases, we can see that blocked goals relate to plunder.

2. Tolkien, *Silmarillion*, 73–77.

THE FACETS OF TROUBLE

For the first man, a bad driver plunders away a sense of community, of loving concern. For the second, what has been plundered is his need to feel absolutely in control.

Helpers must remember to wonder, "What blocked goal lies underneath this person's anger or rage?" Once the goal becomes clear, she must also ask, "Is this goal worthy of a believer in Christ?" For example, let's imagine that a pastor has a married couple in his church where the husband goes on to have many affairs. He hurts his wife and children time after time. In the course of time, the pastor's child befriends one of the unfaithful man's children. The latter comes to the pastor's house many times crying. He has seen his mother weeping over another affair. The pastor feels anger at the man's evil and the pain he causes. He goes to the man and speaks truth to him in the love of Christ, but the man refuses to change. Then the pastor must remember, "Be angry and yet do not sin; do not let the sun go down on your anger, and do not give the devil an opportunity" (Eph 4:26–27).

The pastor's goal is righteous, and so is his anger. His goal is righteous, because he simply wants evil to stop. He also knows that God loves the adulterous man. He hopes that the man will repent and be restored. But the pastor could also have a foolish goal. He could see this situation as an opportunity to play the hero and prove that he deserves respect. Or he could be driven to establish control on his own terms. We must always examine our hearts (Ps 139:23–24).

FORGIVENESS

The story of the unfaithful husband illustrates that many counseling situations involve struggles to forgive. For example, a boy's parents divorced when he was so young that he had no memories of his father. He lived with his mother, who told him many stories describing his father as selfish and unkind. She claimed he never wanted to see the boy. Slowly, the boy's loneliness for his father turned into resentment toward him. After many years—now, he was fifty—he discovered, to his great surprise, that he had an older half brother. Through this brother, the man discovered that his father *had* loved him and that his mother had lied so she could keep the son for herself. She had also destroyed some letters his father had written. The son never saw these testaments of love. The man now felt joy and reached out to his father, only to discover that he had died a year earlier. Oh, how he hated his mother for her lies! How robbed he felt! All chance of knowing his father was stolen by her lies.

His first reaction was complete rage. But then he learned that his mother had been robbed, too. He learned that she had been pregnant by another man when she was eighteen. Her own mother, intensely ambitious, had schemed for her to be rich and have many admirers. She forced her daughter to give up the baby for adoption. The daughter never forgave herself for giving up her firstborn. Becoming depressed, she made many bad choices, became promiscuous, and ended up marrying a criminal who controlled her life completely.

When the man understood the excruciating pain of his mother's life, he saw her with new eyes. Deep inside, the seed of compassion grew. He knew his mother was more than her sin; she needed the grace of forgiveness. Why add to her suffering that of being unforgiven? He came to understand what Rwandan Celestin Musekura expressed: "I began to think of my perpetrators not as beasts and demons but as human beings who, like me, need the power of God to transform their hearts."[3]

Forgiveness becomes easier as we see beyond our pain to the pain of the other. Anyone who causes pain has been born into the pain of a fallen world, just as we have. He or she has suffered the homesickness all of us feel. He or she also has endured wounds that may be deeply buried.

Forgiveness puts the pain of the past behind us. When we forgive, we cancel the debt the other owes for the pain he or she has caused us. "You will pay dearly for that," we hear wounded people say. We don't forgive, because we want to even the score. But then, the other wants to retaliate in turn, and the conflict becomes more and more harsh. Forgiveness breaks the cycle of harshness.

---

3. Jones and Musekura, *Forgiving*, 24–25.

THE FACETS OF TROUBLE

Forgiveness, however, is not the same as excusing someone. For example, a teacher gives a sick child an excuse for missing school. Sickness justifies the child's absence, so an excuse is proper. But a mother could never be justified for lying to her son to keep him from his father. There is no excuse for those lies. Forgiveness pardons what none can excuse. The offender owes a debt, but forgiveness does not collect it. The forgiver remembers that he, too, owes a debt: to God.

Jesus makes forgiveness possible. As Paul reflects, "And be kind to one another, tender-hearted, forgiving each other, just as God in Christ also has forgiven you" (Eph 4:32). Forgiving others rests on the firm foundation that God has forgiven us in Christ. Spiritual conversations should convey to those struggling to forgive that Christ paid dearly but also received abundant blessing in choosing to forgive us. We also pay a price when we forgive, but we also receive the blessing that bitterness will not eat us alive. Someone once observed, "Not forgiving someone is like eating poison and hoping the other guy dies."

Helpers, then, should assist people:

- to remember that we are all wounded and suffering in a fallen world,
- to see the offender as a complicated person who is more than a wrongdoer,
- to cancel the debt,
- to realize one is giving the same gift one has been given by God,
- to grow in thankfulness for Jesus' gift of forgiveness that pours out from God's marvelous grace,
- and to pray for the offender to find the grace of Jesus Christ.

GRIEF

A grieving person experiences sadness over loss and finds that letting go is a deep struggle. Loss reminds us that we live in a world where something goes missing. The unique need of one in grief is to understand what he misses and longs for. When we read about God casting Adam and Eve out of the Garden of Eden, we see what we've lost. God warns them not to take from the tree of life, lest they "eat, and live forever" in their state of sin (Gen 3:22). They would then lose the hope of eternal life. To protect them (and us), God casts them out of their first home. They live now in exile and homelessness. Every loss reminds us of our homesickness. Every loss awakens the wound of exile. What is missing? Home.

Helpers support those in grief by teaching them that sadness reflects our homesickness. Why does this help? Because no one is homesick unless a home exists to be sick for! Just as God sent Israel into exile to purify her in Babylon, so he reminds us that we are "strangers and exiles on the earth." The pangs of exile sharpen our longing for "a better country, that is a heavenly one" (Heb 11:13, 16). When we lose an important person, thing, or status, the pain we feel tells us that we long for home. To our longing, Jesus says:

> Let not your heart be troubled; believe in God, believe also in Me. In My Father's house are many dwelling places; if it were not so, I would have told you; for I go to prepare a place for you. And if I go and prepare a place for you, I will come again, and receive you to Myself, that where I am, there you may be also. (John 14:1–3)

Grief sometimes gets clogged up with other feelings. In the story of the man whose mother lied to him about his father, we can see that she robbed the son of freedom to know and love his father. When his father died, the son's grief was clogged with extra pain about a missed opportunity. The door to his father had been unlocked all along, but he didn't know it. In such situations, helpers need to invite the grieving one to talk about the feelings that add extra burdens to their grief. Those who come alongside others can use the sections of this book that apply to those specific feelings to help the grieving person.

THE FACETS OF TROUBLE
CHAPTER 6 QUESTIONS

1. Marriage is not a relationship for meeting needs and controlling risk. How would you design ways to help marriages focus on giving, not taking? How would you design ways to help people take the risks involved in loving?

2. "Forgiveness is easier when we see beyond our pain to the pain of the other." How would you help people have a greater compassion for those who have hurt them? How would you deal with the great pain that wounded people often feel?

3. How can pain show us that we are homesick? How does pain show us what kind of world we are made for? How can you help others trust God and hope in his gift of life that extends into homegoing?

CHAPTER 7

Traumatic Stress

Helpers who encounter people under traumatic stress should know that working with them is like running a marathon.[1] According to Judith Herman, healing from trauma involves three stages: establishing safety, remembrance and mourning, and reconnecting to oneself and others.[2] Let's think about Sarah here. She needs to feel safe in two ways: first, she needs safety in her physical environment; second, in her relationship with her helper.

The helper should ask whether Sarah feels safe where she lives. If she does not, the helper may need to enlist family and/or church support to find Sarah a safe place to live. As the two engage in spiritual conversations, Sarah may struggle to trust the helper. The one who helps should expect this struggle. After all, one should be able to trust an uncle, right? Yet, her uncle made Sarah's body his plaything. Will the helper use her in some way? Or will she keep Sarah's best interests always in mind?

UNDERSTANDING TRAUMA

The brain supports the mind. For the brain to be a good support, it must be healthy. When the brain suffers, mental health suffers.

1. Herman, *Trauma and Recovery*, 174.
2. Herman, *Trauma and Recovery*, 156.

TRAUMATIC STRESS

Trauma is a force that is truly harmful on the brain. Trauma is any sudden event that endangers life and health. Examples of trauma include a military assault on civilians, an earthquake, sexual or physical abuse, a tornado, an automobile accident, combat, rape. All of these are traumatic events. How does trauma affect the brain?

1. It makes the brain more likely to see threat where there is no threat.
2. It causes the brain to be hypersensitive to stress.
3. It makes it hard for the brain to discern what is important and what is unimportant.[3]

Imagine a combat veteran who has returned home. He is walking down the street on a perfectly normal day when he hears a loud bang. Normally, his brain would know the sound is an explosion in an old car engine. But the trauma of combat causes his brain to receive the bang as an exploding bomb. He dives to the ground and curls into a ball. It may take him a long time to remember that he is safe. It may take a long time as well for the stress in his body and mind to return to normal. He may need a period of peace and quiet, or he may need to exercise or find a trusted person with whom he can talk.

Trauma uniquely features an overwhelmed coping ability. Trauma brings too great a load, as if someone tried to stuff a battleship into a shoebox. In traumatic stress, this condition shows up in numbness and intrusion. The traumatized person may feel very little. But when something (like the car engine backfiring) triggers the trauma, the feelings become too intense to handle; and the body takes over, reacting powerfully.

The counselor should take a history of trauma from every person who comes for counseling. Some questions to ask include:

- Have you ever been in combat?
- Have you been in a vehicle wreck?
- Did anyone beat you when you were a child?

3. van der Kolk, *Body Keeps the Score*, 2–3.

UNSTUCK

- Has anyone sexually abused or raped you?
- Have you ever experienced a severe storm and feared for your life?
- Have you ever feared for your life in some other way?

These are hard questions, but they help show the helper whether she may need to change her way of approaching the suffering one. Trauma affects both the brain and the body. We pointed out some effects on the brain above. The body changes as it tries to contain the intense suffering without screaming or shutting down. One's body may feel stiff or numb or agitated. "The past is alive in the form of gnawing interior discomfort."[4] One can become a stranger to his or her own body. In such cases, the helper can teach the person ways to quiet the body (see the exercise in the next paragraph, for example). Please note that methods to quiet the body will only work after the traumatized one feels safe. Again, a person like Sarah must feel safe where she lives and safe with the helper.

Sarah's body must be helped to feel a sense of "Sabbath." The helper might take her through the three verses of Ps 131 in the following way:

- "O Lord, my heart is not proud, / nor my eyes haughty; / Nor do I involve myself in great matters, / Or in things too difficult for me" (Ps 131:1). The helper can have Sarah close her eyes while the helper reads this verse and then prays something like, "Father, help your child not to shoulder the 'great matter' of what she thinks she should have done differently in response to the trauma. Help her to have mercy on herself, not loading herself with things 'too difficult' for her."
- "Surely I have composed and quieted my soul; / Like a weaned child rests against his mother, / My soul is like a weaned child within me" (Ps 131:2). Again, read the verse to Sarah as her eyes are closed. Then pray, "Jesus, may this child of yours rest in your arms. I pray that your quiet and calm heart will be a resting place for the unrest and ache and sorrow in Sarah's

---

4. van der Kolk, *Body Keeps the Score*, 96.

soul. May her body find in you a space where painful tears meet peaceful assurance of your love."

- "O Israel, hope in the Lord / From this time forth and forever" (Ps 131:3). After reading this verse to the hurting one, pray, "Holy Spirit of God, grant hope to Sarah, who has suffered. May your future come with warm outreach and holding. May you come from beyond the pain to contain it so that the pain itself realizes it is not infinite. May the pain find its limits in you so Sarah can rest."

Calming exercises like this should be repeated as needed. This helps give the body permission to live in "Sabbath." Dallas Willard says, "The capacity to simply be, to rest, would remove one from most of the striving that leads to misery." He goes on to say that the ability to be still and to rest "comes to fullness only when it reaches our body. Peace is a condition of the body, and until it has enveloped our body it has not enveloped us. Peace comes to our body when it is at home in the rightness and power of God."[5]

Prayer is where the body finds this sense of Sabbath. We need to sit quietly before the Lord and hear him speak his yes of love over us. God's yes brings even our bodies to the place where the trauma can become as a child crying. Slowly, the crying and terrified child within our trauma feels the power and comfort of this yes from God. Like the weaned child in Ps 131, the trauma begins to ease. Our hurt souls and bodies find comfort in God's yes of love, and they rest on God like a child on its mother (Ps 131:2). The shift from trauma as a child crying to trauma as easing into rest may take many sessions of discussion and prayer. Again, this shift will only be possible if the traumatized person feels safe.

Someone once said, "What the mind cannot hold overflows into the body." What bothers the mind can indeed show up in the body. But this often is not clear, because the mind and body don't effectively work together after trauma. Their separation complicates this truth that mental pain overflows into the body. Instead of "talking" to the mind, the body sends signals out into the world, giving clues through the ways we behave. We act out our pain without

---

5. Willard, *Renovation of the Heart*, 174.

words, communicating through our behavior. One's body may communicate trauma through

- poor eye contact
- overdressing or dressing provocatively
- slumped posture
- being easily startled
- fits of rage
- silence or constant talking
- addictive habits (like drinking, using drugs, or gambling).

The body's calming may take a long time. The helper must expect ongoing questions about the safety of the helping relationship. He or she must keep working to become a safe person. The main ways to become safe are, first, to use the questions about trauma listed above. When the person seeking help hears them, he or she may begin to believe that the helper may be able to handle the pain. Second, remember to be a good listener. Listening well is equivalent to loving well. Listening well creates a feeling of safety. When a person knows the helper provides true listening, hope rises. The love of Christ brings healing power, but that love cannot move through an unsafe person.

Third, a safe helper knows and understands her own pain. Nothing will awaken our inner pain like hearing another's trauma. The extreme suffering of others requires that we suffer with them. If we have ignored our own life's suffering, we will feel anxiety when another's pain comes near.

Fourth, go slowly. Approaches that are too rushed or intense will tempt the traumatized person to shut down. The wise helper does not hurry the trauma victim too quickly into painful memories. It may take a long time for the suffering person to learn to tolerate what he or she felt during the trauma. If we don't go slowly, we may unintentionally cause *more* trauma by pushing too quickly into the trauma.

A wise helper will assist the trauma victim in connecting her depression, anxiety, and/or anger to the fact that she has suffered

TRAUMATIC STRESS

trauma. People like Sarah don't automatically make this connection. This simple realization can be a great help. For a person to be able to say, "I am depressed, because I was sexually abused," helps that one not to feel as crazy and alone. A depressed or anxious person may worry about why she feels the way she feels. Knowing that past trauma connects to anxiety and depression eases a great burden.

CHAPTER 7 QUESTIONS

1. "Prayer is where the body finds this sense of Sabbath. We need to sit quietly before the Lord and hear him speak his yes of love over us." Put these thoughts in your own words. How would you use these ideas to help a traumatized person?

2. Review the four points above about the counselor's being a safe person. For each point, write down a strength and a weakness of your own. For example, point one refers you to the chapter's questions for evaluating trauma. Are there questions on this list you would feel less comfortable asking? Are there those that are more comfortable? For each of the four points, take these strengths and weaknesses to the Lord in prayer. Ask him for his instruction about how to strengthen your strengths and shore up your weaknesses.

CHAPTER 8

What I Have Learned as a Helper

After three and a half years as a pastor, I became more curious about why people behave as they do. I went back to seminary, got a degree in counseling, and became a licensed counselor.[1] In that capacity, I've been helping people with their problems for over thirty years. What have I learned?

First, I've learned that I must center my counseling on the cross of Jesus Christ. The apostle Paul said, "For I determined to know nothing among you except Jesus Christ, and Him crucified" (1 Cor 2:2). He took his stand on the cross: "For it is written, 'I will destroy the wisdom of the wise, / And the cleverness of the clever I will set aside'" (1 Cor 1:19, quoting Isa 29:14). I will not help people with the wisdom of the world (which pushes God aside). I will not help people through my cleverness. I will help people most when I can help them see that their flesh pretends to be wise and clever by saying, "I can make life work apart from God" or "I can make life work by working my way to God." It would take a god to work one's way to God. As soon as we decide to be the god of our lives, we are on the

---

1. Although I will, of necessity, use the terms "counselor" and "counseling" in this brief chapter, every lesson discussed applies to the term "helper" that I've been using throughout this book.

WHAT I HAVE LEARNED AS A HELPER

road to developing mental-health problems—i.e., our minds begin to crack under the strain of taking on the God role.

Second, I have learned that I must go where people struggle. I cannot stand at a distance and tell them what to do. I must "weep with those who weep" (Rom 12:15). If I weep with them, if I listen patiently, if I seek to understand as intently as they want to be understood, I stand a chance of helping by God's grace. African writer Eshetu Abate says, "Almost everywhere in the world, people are looking for self-giving love, someone who will help them in their suffering and agony.... [Therefore] we must engage in self-giving and sacrificial love in the discipleship of the cross."[2] I've learned that I cannot play it safe in counseling. I must risk the trauma of hearing the true pain of the other's heart. I must risk the defensiveness that may come when I speak into the other's foolish ways of handling his or her pain. My safety must come from Christ. My friend and mentor Larry Crabb once commended this truth to me: "I am significant and secure in Jesus Christ and whatever he chooses to provide."[3] Whether Jesus provides much besides himself or *only* himself, we are secure in him, because he tells such a large story of hope that we can shelter in it always. I have tried to practice this. It is a challenge to keep it in mind.

Third, I have learned that everyone has a story that has formed and de-formed him or her. Counseling involves helping a person remember and understand the story one has lived so far. Our stories act as the hands of a weaver, but often the tapestry is hanging in a back room. We do not understand the pattern of our lives. Counseling must bring the tapestry into the light and help others see their hidden patterns of living.

Finally, I have learned that the church too often bypasses mental health (the renewing of the mind at penetrating depth) in favor of behavioral health. That is, keeping the rules becomes more important than a deeply penetrating holiness. Self-effort to obey glorifies us, while true, Spirit-led changes of heart show us that we

---

2. Abate, "Theology of the Cross," 130.

3. Dr. Crabb spoke these words many times in class during his tenure as chairman of the Biblical Counseling Department at Grace Theological Seminary.

are beggars who need the Lord all day, every day. Obedience is still the goal, but a thankful, humble obedience rather than an anxious, prideful striving. Counseling works to foster an openness to God's stripping away the pride, anxiety, and sensuality that interfere with our mental and spiritual health.

Conclusion

This book focuses on the importance of the helper's growing in Christ. We cannot take anyone one inch farther than we have progressed. This book is, in part, a call for helpers to redouble their love for and commitment to the Lord. Not only must helpers examine their relationship with God, they must also look carefully at their relationships with others. Love God and love people! These are the two greatest commandments (Matt 22:37–40). Love drives us to increase our efforts to join those who come to us.

We must listen and learn about the wilderness that holds others captive. We learn to quiet ourselves so we can hear others and hear the Lord in our hearts. A noisy soul can offer but poor help! As we hear others, we pray to discern ways to lead them onto a new map. This new map has the "landmarks" of God's kingdom. Some of the landmarks are love, joy, peace, patience, kindness, gentleness, goodness, faithfulness, and self-control (Gal 5:22–23). We help others see how their flesh patterns get in the way, hindering the work of the Spirit.

Through the joy and work of repentance, we help them move past these hindrances. As we ourselves learn not to quench the Spirit, we help them give him free rein in their own lives. As they "keep on being filled with the Spirit" (Eph 5:18b, my translation), they "walk by the Spirit" and do not "carry out the desires of the flesh" (Gal 5:16). This increase of the Spirit releases new energy to "walk in newness of life" (Rom 6:4). The spiritual practices (prayer, Bible study, etc.) are the "pots" we set out in the "rain" of the Holy Spirit so that this newness may continue. We become renewed people, ever renewing. Through this journey, God progressively forms us in the image of Christ (Gal 4:19).

Bibliography

Abate, Eshetu. "The Theology of the Cross in the African Context." In *The Theology of the Cross for the 21st Century*, edited by Alberto L. Garcia and A. R. Victor Raj, 121–37. St. Louis: Concordia, 2002.
Abbott-Smith, G. *A Manual Greek Lexicon of the New Testament*. Edinburgh: T. & T. Clark, 1973.
American Psychiatric Association. *Diagnostic and Statistical Manual of Mental Disorders*. 5th ed. Arlington, VA: American Psychiatric Association, 2013.
Anderson, Ray S. *Christians Who Counsel*. Grand Rapids: Zondervan, 1990.
Argyris, Chris. *Reasoning, Learning, and Action*. San Francisco: Jossey-Bass, 1982.
Barnes, Jonathan. "Psyche." In *The Oxford Companion to the Mind*, edited by Richard L. Gregory, 648–49. Gregory. Oxford: Oxford University Press, 1987.
Barth, Karl. *The Doctrine of Reconciliation*. Vol. 4, pt. 3, half-vol. 1 of *Church Dogmatics*. Translated by Geoffrey Bromiley. Edinburgh: T. & T. Clark, 1961.
Bauer, Walter, et al. *A Greek-English Lexicon of the New Testament and Other Early Christian Literature*. Chicago: University of Chicago Press, 1957.
Brown, Francis, et al. *A Hebrew and English Lexicon of the Old Testament*. Oxford: Oxford University Press, 1977.
Brueggemann, Walter. *Cadences of Home: Preaching among Exiles*. Louisville: Westminster John Knox, 1997.
———. *The Psalms and the Life of Faith*. Minneapolis: Fortress, 1995.
Bruner, Frederick Dale. *The Gospel of John: A Commentary*. Grand Rapids: Eerdmans, 2012.
Casement, Patrick J. *Learning from the Patient*. New York: Guilford, 1985.
Complete Wordfinder. Pleasantville, NY: Readers Digest, 1996.
Congar, Yves. *I Believe in the Holy Spirit*. Vol. 3. New York: Seabury, 1983.
Crabb, Larry. *Inside-Out*. Colorado Springs, CO: NavPress, 2007.
———. "School of Spiritual Direction." Unpublished lecture notes presented at the School of Spiritual Direction conference 57 of New Way Ministries, Asheville, NC, April 18–23, 2015.

BIBLIOGRAPHY

Crabb, Lawrence J. *Effective Biblical Counseling*. Grand Rapids: Zondervan, 1977.

Dawson, Gerrit Scott. *Called by a New Name: Becoming What God Has Promised*. Nashville: Upper Room, 1997.

Earle, Samantha. "What is the Social Imaginary?" Social Imaginaries Project. https://socialimaginaries.org/the-imaginary-system-of-society/.

Gerkin, Charles V. *The Living Human Document*. Nashville: Abingdon, 1984.

Hayes, Stephen C., and Spencer Smith. *Get Out of Your Mind and into Your Life: The New Acceptance and Commitment Therapy*. Oakland, CA: New Harbinger, 2005.

Heidegger, Martin. *Being and Time*. Translated by John Macquarrie and Edward Robinson. New York: Harper & Row, 1962.

Herman, Judith. *Trauma and Recovery: The Aftermath of Violence—From Domestic Abuse to Political Terror*. New York: Basic, 1997.

Hobbes, Thomas. *Of Man, Being the First Part of Leviathan*. In *French and English Philosophers*, edited by Charles W. Eliot, 307–417. The Harvard Classics 34. New York: P. F. Collier & Son, 1910.

John of the Cross. *The Living Flame of Love*. Translated by E. Allison Peers. New York: Triumph, 1977.

Jones, L. Gregory, and Celestin Musekura. *Forgiving as We've Been Forgiven: Community Practices for Making Peace*. Downers Grove, IL: InterVarsity, 2010.

Käsemann, Ernst. *Jesus Means Freedom*. Translated by Frank Clarke. Philadelphia: Fortress, 1970.

Kidner, Derek. *A Time to Mourn and a Time to Dance: The Message of Ecclesiastes*. Downers Grove, IL: InterVarsity, 1976.

Koehler, Ludwig, et al. *The Hebrew and Aramaic Lexicon of the Old Testament*. Translated by M. E. J. Richardson. Boston: Brill, 2001.

Lacugna, Catherine Mowry. *God for Us: The Trinity and Christian Life*. San Francisco: HarperSanFrancisco, 1973.

Lovelace, Richard F. *Dynamics of Spiritual Life: An Evangelical Theology of Renewal*. Downers Grove, IL: InterVarsity, 1979.

Marchant, J. R. V., and Joseph F. Charles. *Cassell's Latin Dictionary*. New York: Funk & Wagnalls, 1958.

Moltmann, Jurgen. *The Trinity and the Kingdom*. Translated by Margaret Kohl. Minneapolis: Fortress, 1993.

Owen, John. "Of Temptation." In *Temptation and Sin*, 88–151. Vol. 6 of *The Works of John Owen*, edited by William Goold. Carlisle, PA: Banner of Truth, 1995.

Ricoeur, Paul. *Time and Narrative*. Vol. 1. Translated by Kathleen McLaughlin and David Pellauer. Chicago: University of Chicago Press, 1984.

Shores, Stephen D. "An Exploration of the Image of God and the Flesh as Bases for a Biblical Counseling Model." DMin thesis, Gordon-Conwell Theological Seminary, 1999.

BIBLIOGRAPHY

Strupp, Hans, and Jeffrey Binder. *Psychotherapy in a New Key: A Guide to Time-Limited Dynamic Psychotherapy.* New York: Basic, 1984.

Taylor, Charles. *Modern Social Imaginaries.* Durham, NC: Duke University Press, 2004.

Tolkien, J. R. R. *The Silmarillion.* Boston: Houghton Mifflin, 1977.

van der Kolk, Bessel. *The Body Keeps the Score: Brain, Mind, and Body in the Healing of Trauma.* New York: Viking, 2014.

Weiser, Artur. *The Psalms: A Commentary.* Translated by Herbert Hartwell. Philadelphia: Westminster, 1962.

Willard, Dallas. *Renovation of the Heart.* Colorado Springs, CO: NavPress, 2002.

Wolff, Hans Walter. *Anthropology of the Old Testament.* Mifflintown, PA: Sigler, 1996.

www.ingramcontent.com/pod-product-compliance
Lightning Source LLC
Chambersburg PA
CBHW070510090426
42735CB00012B/2724